Textile/Garment Screen Printing

Fourth Edition

by

Albert Kosloff, M.A.

Technical Consultant, Honorary Member
of Screen Printing Association
International, and Member of Academy
of Screen Printing Technology

ST Publications
Cincinnati, Ohio

Published by ST Publications, 407 Gilbert
Avenue, Cincinnati, Ohio 45202

Library of Congress Cataloging-in-Publication Data

Kosloff, Albert.
    Textile/garment screen printing.

    Includes bibliographical references and index.
    1. Screen process printing.   2. Textile printing.
I. Title.
TT273.K67   1987   667'.38   86-27972
ISBN 0-911380-76-0

Printed in the United States of America.

To Esther, David, Nina and Sandy

Preface

The constant growth of screen printing or mitography in the United States and in various parts of the world, especially since 1965, is an affirmation of faith in the future of the industry. As is true of other dynamic industries, one of the greatest barriers to understanding in the areas of research and product development is a lack of communication. Thus, the challenge is to extend growth by communicating the results of objective evaluation and of the new knowledge made available through research in screen printing and in related fields. The attainment of such an objective is only realized if more screen printers, textile printers, general printers, individuals who sell and purchase printing, educators, students and any other individuals interested in the vocational or avocational pursuit of the field are cognizant of the potential of textile and general screen printing.

Research in the textile screen-printing industry and in related industries, development of automated and semi-automatic screen-printing equipment, screen-printing dyes, plastisols, sublimation dyes and other inks and transfer printing have universally accelerated the growth and expanded the markets of textile screen printing. This growth has produced greater activity in the general and specialized textile screen-printing shop and has also stressed to this writer the importance of presenting standardized newer processes for this fourth revision of the book *Textile/Garment Screen Printing*. The versatility of the process in being able to print on any material, shape, surface or size and with so many types of inks also stresses the continual need for more data and information on this specific phase of screen printing.

The author expresses gratitude to *Screen Printing* magazine and *Signs of the Times* magazine for their permission to use material and illustrations which the writer has contributed to past issues of the publications;

to the editors of the above journals; to the publisher—Signs of the Times for its courtesies; and to his wife for her tolerance in allowing our home to become a screen-printing laboratory where so many creative individuals have met through the years.

It has been a privilege for this writer to have been part of the growth and development of screen printing and to have worked with the following firms and individuals on different phases of screen printing. He is grateful for their help and interest: ABA Organization, Chicago, Illinois; ABC Photo Supply Corporation, Paterson, NJ; Advance Process Supply Co., Chicago, Illinois; American Crayon Co., Sandusky, Ohio; Associated Chemical Companies, Ltd., Harrogate, Yorkshire, England; Atlas Silk Screen Supply Co., Chicago, IL; Castle Prints, Inc., Washington, DC; Cellusuede Products, Inc., Rockford, Illinois; Chicago Art Institute, Chicago, Illinois; Chicago Silk Screen Supply Co., Chicago, Illinois; Ciba-Geigy Corp., Greensboro, NC; Cincinnati Printing and Drying Systems, Inc., Cincinnati, Ohio; Colonial Printing Ink Co., East Rutherford, NJ; Cooper Graphics, Niagara Falls, NY; Dalso Athletic Company, Inc., Dallas, Texas; Douthitt Co., Detroit, MI; Excello, Ltd., Chicago, IL; Flocking Equipment Manufacturing Co., Los Angeles, CA; Foremost Screen Print, Garfield, NJ; Erika Golliher, Project Editor; Hydro Prints, Charlotte, NC; Imperial Chemical Industries, Ltd., Manchester, England; Indev, Inc., Pawtucket, RI; Inmont Corp., Hawthorne, NJ; Jungfrau, Inc., Cedar Grove, NJ; Kopal Industries, Seabrook, Texas; Lawson Printing Machine, St. Louis, MO; M and M Research, Oshkosh, WI; Naz-Dar Company, Chicago, Illinois; Northern Dyeing Corp., Washington, DC; nuArc Company, Chicago, Illinois; Penncraft, Inc., Rosemont, Illinois; Photolith International, Scranton, PA; Precision Screen Machines, Inc., Hawthorne, NJ; Printed Fabrics, Carrollton, GA; Ranar Manufacturing Co., Los Angeles, CA; Richardson Industries Corp., Columbus, Ohio; Screen Printing Association International, Fairfax, Virginia; Screen Printing Magazine, Cincinnati, Ohio; Carole Singleton, Book Division Coordinator; Societe Alsaciene Constructions Mecaniques, Cambridge, MA; Stork Brabant, Boxmeer, Holland; Textile Industries Magazine, Atlanta, GA; Tower Iron Works, Inc., Deekong, MA; Joseph Ulano, New York, NY; Ulano Products, Inc., New York, NY; Union Ink Co., Ridgefield, NJ; and Vastex Co., Inc., Somerville, NJ.

Albert Kosloff

CONTENTS

Chapter I

TEXTILE SCREEN PRINTING

A process or a phase of an industry does not live in a vacuum; neither does it emerge suddenly. Generally it is influenced and governed by socioeconomic factors, by the needs it must answer and by the technology of related processes. Often the pioneer must start with related processes in order to develop new techniques. While screen printing differs from the other methods of decorating textiles, it has been influenced by them. Therefore, in order to have a more complete understanding of textile screen printing, the printer should have a general knowledge of the other methods which have been and are being used to decorate, print and dye textile surfaces. This knowledge may lead to a better appreciation, on the part of the printer and the novice, of the advantages, problems, challenges and potential of screen-printing on textiles.

Basically, screen printing, like all dyeing and printing on textiles, is a method of decorating materials. The art of dyeing has been known and practiced for centuries. The discovery in England of aniline dye (or aniline purple) by William Henry Perkins in 1856, when he was trying to make quinine from a coal tar derivative known as aniline, was the starting point of the modern coal-tar dye industry. The thousands of synthetic dyes which have been developed since then have placed even more emphasis on the use of dyeing and textile printing.

Dyeing is a process by which a color of relative permanency and uniformity is produced on a material. The colored substance which has an affinity for fixes and which gives color to the fabric is known as a dye or a pigment. Chemically, dyes are complex compounds dissolved in solutions. Today most of them are synthetic. Pigments are insoluble in the vehicle or medium in which they are mixed and are suspended in a solution. A dye, therefore, is a color-producing substance in solution which is absorbed by the textile fiber from that solution. Although

1

textile surfaces that are screen-printed with pigment-type dyes or screen-printing inks may appear to be dyed, the printed areas are really bonded to the surface by mechanical means in a synthetic or other vehicle. For example, much screen-printing on textiles is done with water-in-oil emulsions and oil-in-water emulsions as illustrated in Figure 1.

Textiles are fabrics (cloth materials) obtained from yarn by weaving, felting, knitting, braiding, netting, knotting or some other interlacing process. The fabric may be made of natural or synthetic fibers. Fibers are classified into animal types (wool, silk, vicuna); vegetable types (linen or cotton); synthetic fibers (nylon, orlon, dacron); mineral types (fiberglass); and combinations of the above. Because the dyeing of each type of fiber is carried out somewhat differently, it is a complex process and industry. Before starting to print a dye on a fabric, it is necessary for the processor to identify the fiber of which the material is composed.

Although fabrics are colored by various means, generally in dyeing, the color is applied to the fabric through or around the stationary material. In textile printing, the dye ink (or dye paste) may be brought to the material, or the material may move past a unit that contains the

Figure 1. Attractive terry-cloth items in matching design in center, and dishtowels in cotton fabric printed with different designs at each side, are all screen-printed mechanically with screen process oil-in-water emulsions. The screen printing, drying and heat-curing was accomplished automatically. (Courtesy of Excello Ltd., Chicago, IL)

color. Textile printing is also a method of dyeing. In printing, the dye is applied in paste form as design patterns on the cloth, or as restricted printed areas not covering the whole fabric. While there are other methods of classifying textile printing, it is usually classified according to the method employed in printing. The following are printing methods which decorate fabrics and at the same time produce dyeing: (1) roller (or machine) printing; (2) screen printing (or mitography*); (3) block printing; (4) spray (or stencil) printing; (5) batik printing; (6) discharge printing; (7) resist printing; (8) photographic printing; and (9) heat-transfer printing which is dealt with in Chapters XI and XIII.

Of the above methods, roller printing, screen printing and heat-transfer printing are the most important industrially and commercially. Block printing and stencil printing are used for short runs, sample printings and for artistic and avocational pursuits. Block printing has been replaced commercially by screen printing, because the latter process can produce the same effects and print much larger areas. Resist and discharge printing are sometimes used in textile printing and can be done manually or mechanically.

While some screen printers may make a distinction between printing on garments such as T-shirts, dresswear and caps, and other types of screen printing, if these products are screen-printed, garment printing is a part of screen printing.

Block Printing

Wood, linoleum, rubber, metal or composition blocks are used for reproducing designs in textile printing. The desired designs are carved on the surface so that the printing patterns are in relief, similar to letter-press printing. While printing is usually done manually, it has been done mechanically in England and France on a machine known as the Perroting printing machine. Should screen printers attempt to do block printing in order to acquaint themselves with the process, they will find that the block will absorb more ink (or dye) for printing, if the printing surfaces in relief are first covered with flock. The application of flock involves rolling on a flock adhesive with a roller (or brayer) to the relief parts of the block and then sifting a solid coating of flock onto the adhesive-covered areas. Flock is finely-cut rayon, wool, cotton or synthetic fibers of length sizes varying from about 1/2 mm. to 1/4". The subject is covered more completely in Chapter XVI.

An interesting way to reproduce block printing by means of screen-

*The term **mitography** (mi tog' ra fi) was coined by this writer in 1942 with the objective of offering a term that is comprehensive, concise, technically correct and easy to translate into other languages. The word was taken from the Greek prefix **mitos** meaning "threads or fibers" and the suffix **graphein** meaning "to write or print." **Photomitography** refers to the photographic processes of screen process printing.

printing is to take the carved block, cover the relief parts with tusche (a greasy wax-like substance), and stamp the tusche-covered block on the inside of the screen fabric of the printing screen. When a tusche-glue or tusche-lacquer screen like this is prepared, the screen will reproduce block-printing designs. The screen printing may be done manually or mechanically. (Tusche-type printing screens are covered in Chapter VII.)

Stencil or Spray Printing

In stencil (or spray) printing the color is sprayed, dabbed, brushed or sponged onto the material through a stencil which has been prepared on a thin sheet of metal, plastic, cardboard or waterproof transparent paper. According to historians, the stencil was used in very early cultures; its use has not changed in principle.

Screen printing employs a more interesting and modern method of the stencil principle. In screen printing it is possible to use a printing screen in place of a stencil, holding the screen snugly against a material (or surface) on which it may be difficult to print, with the color sprayed through the design areas of the screen. This is a practical technique to use on absorbent surfaces such as velvet or foam rubber, and for obtaining better detail in spraying. Dyestuffs used for spraying are in solution in water, alcohol or another solvent. Alcohol has a tendency to dry quicker and thus eliminates running of the color at the stencil edges. Stencil spraying may also be used to supplement screen printing in producing unusual shading effects on textile materials.

Batik Printing

Batik printing, a Javanese hand method for producing designs on fabrics, was introduced to Europe by the Dutch in the 1640s; although it is maintained by historians that this technique was used long before that time. Batik printing is similar to resist printing in that it employs a waxy material or a special paste to prevent the dye from penetrating the cloth. The design to be reproduced is drawn on the undyed cloth with a tool known as a "tjanting" or is stamped with a stamp known as a "tjap." The tool (or stamp) applies the wax or resist. The fabric is first immersed in lukewarm water, because dyes may streak if applied to dry material. The fabric is then immersed in a low-temperature dye solution, or the dye is brushed over the fabric. The areas with wax on them resist the dye and remain the original color of the cloth. After the dyed material is dried, steamed and finished, the wax resist is removed by the application of heat or with a solvent. One way to remove wax is to wrap the cloth in absorbent paper so that the paper will absorb the wax during the steaming of the cloth. Multicolor decorations may be done with batik dyeing, the process being repeated for each color printed. Lighter colors are generally printed first.

4

The manual reproduction of batik designs is very costly and slow. Commercially it can be done by roller printing and screen printing. Batik printing has been done by screen-printing a resist solution on the cloth. After dyeing, the screen-printed resist is removed by dissolving it with a solvent recommended by the manufacturer of the resist. The advantage of screen printing is evident, as varied printing screens may be employed to produce complex or detailed designs and sharper printing. Also, the screens may be used over and over, while designs drawn by hand onto cloth must each be done individually and are not easily duplicated.

Discharge Printing

In discharge (or extract) printing, a darker-colored dyed fabric is printed with a chemical compound that destroys, discharges or extracts the dye from the darker ground color. The method removes dye from the desired areas of the dyed fabric, leaving other areas colorless or white. If desired, rather that printing the discharge paste on the cloth, it may be applied by stenciling or painting. Discharging is done to obtain a lighter area so that a color lighter than the ground color may be printed in that particular spot (or spots). Because dyes are transparent, printing a light color on top of a dark color will produce a combination of the two colors rather than the desired lighter color. In discharge printing, the original ground color must be printed or dyed with a dyestuff that can be discharged. Discharge printing may be done just to produce the exposed original color of the cloth, or a lighter color may be applied at the same time as the discharge paste to produce the designs of the desired color. Discharge printing is discussed in more detail in Chapter XV.

Resist Printing

In resist printing, the undyed fabric is printed with a substance known as a resist. The resist, like the waxy material in batik dyeing, prevents the dye from penetrating the cloth in the printed areas. The resist is removed after the cloth has been dyed, leaving a pattern of the original color of the cloth on the dyed color. In the discharge method, the fabric is first dyed and then the darker ground color is extracted by printing a discharge paste.

The *tie-and-dye* method of dye decorating uses the resist-dyeing method by knotting, binding, folding or sewing parts of the cloth in such a way that when the total piece of cloth is dyed, the dye will not penetrate the tied or bound parts of the cloth. Tie-dye designs may be reproduced in quantity by screen process printing on textile materials.

Photographic Printing

Photographic textile printing involves coating (or sensitizing) the fabric with a chemical that is sensitive to light, and exposing the fabric to a negative or positive containing the design, by means of a contact (or photographic) projection. It is similar to printing photographs on photographic paper. Varied types of photographs, including colored reproductions, may be reproduced on textile material.

Many of the direct photographic screen-printing emulsions may be coated onto the cloth in a similar fashion to the preparation of printing screens. When the coat (or coats) is dried and exposed to actinic light, then washed-out, an emulsion-impregnated cloth is obtained with copy or an illustration on the cloth. This writer has used the latter technique to produce various types of images on cloth.

Roller Machine Printing

Roller machine printing is the leading industrial textile-printing process which produces billions of yards of printed cloth annually in the United States and other countries. It is a method of printing on fabrics with printing rollers, usually engraved copper or chromium- plated copper rollers. The engraving is an intaglio process, since the design areas are below the surface of the roller, similar to that employed in rotogravure.

As illustrated in the simple drawing in Figure 2, the printing machine consists essentially of a large-diameter cylinder, the diameter being determined by the number of printing rollers around the cylinder. Each printing roller around the circumference of the large cylinder is a unit consisting of (1) an engraved printing roller on which the pattern to be printed is produced; (2) a furnishing roller which is partially submerged in a print-paste trough or a color box, and which transfers the print-paste to the printing roller; (3) a cleaning doctor (or blade) for removing material that adheres to the surface, leaving the dye paste in the engraved portions of the printing roller; and (4) a lint doctor (or blade). As the furnishing roller turns, it transfers the correct amount of color from the trough to the printing roller.

Roller printing is done on machines which may have as many as fourteen printing rollers, one roller being needed for each color printed. As illustrated in Figure 2, the print machine cylinder is covered with layers—a layer of fabric to be printed, a back grey cloth and a blanket. The back grey cloth is a soft cotton material that is fed into the machine with the fabric to be printed, and serves to protect the blanket from being contaminated. After the fabric has passed through the printing roller, the layers are separated and the printed cloth goes through a drying process, either through a drying chamber or around drying cans. Some machines are now using rubber and rubberized blankets instead of the back grey material. The blankets leave the machine automatically, are washed, dried and go back to the machine to be used again. The cloth

6

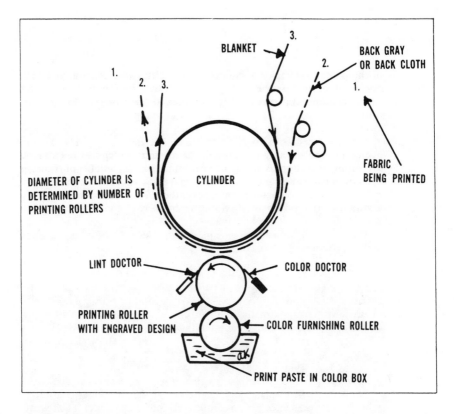

Figure 2. The principle of machine roller textile printing.

to be printed passes around the main cylinder, and comes in contact with the print roller, if one color is to be printed, and with rollers if multicolor work is being done. As the engraved (or printing) roller rotates, it applies the dye paste from the etched-out portions of the roller. The area of the pattern printed equals the length of the roller times its circumference.

The lint blade (or doctor) is applied to the surface of the print roller after it leaves contact with the cloth. The lint doctor removes the coloring material or loose fibers on the surface of the roller so that the dye material is not carried into the paste box or the color box. On modern machines there are other methods of removing color material from the printing roller. These varied parts of the roller- printing machine are synchronized so that all the processes are done automatically and sequentially.

It is evident that planning and adjusting for printing the color sequences requires skill on the part of the machine operator. The machine, the type of patterns being printed, the fabric being printed, the pressure

7

of the print roller against the cylinder, the thickness and angle of the doctor blade against the print roller, the dye and the emotional state of the printing craftsman—all these factors affect the results in roller printing.

When it is necessary to print sample designs before investing in labor, in engraved rollers and in printing large-volume yardage for textile consumption, textile mills and roller machine printing establishments are beginning to employ screen printing more and more. The principle of printing a design through a screen, and the various other advantages of textile screen printing are covered in the next chapter.

Figures 3 and 4 illustrate some interesting examples of screen- printed textile products.

Figure 3. Exhibit of students' textile screen printing done manually with tusche-glue and other types of printing screens. (Courtesy of The American Crayon Co., Sandusky, Ohio and Chicago Art Institute, Chicago, IL)

Figure 4. Satin ribbons for display purposes have been printed with oil-vehicle screen-printing inks. (Courtesy of Chief Display Print Corp., Chicago, IL)

Chapter II

THE PRINCIPLE OF TEXTILE SCREEN PRINTING

One of the first items screen-printed in the United States was the felt banner, in about 1910. In 1924 U.S. Patent 1,494,798 for a stencil apparatus (similar to the modern textile screen-printing table) was issued to Joseph J. Odajian of Manhattan. There was some textile screen printing done in the 1930s, but it was the years after World War II which brought the greatest increase in textile screen printing. Prior to the war, textile printing was done in the general screen-printing shop on such materials as denim, sign cloth, cotton, burlap, canvas and felt, with flexible screen-process lacquers, opaque colors, oil-vehicle inks and screen-process enamels. After the war, some firms started doing screen-printing on silk, wool and drapery materials for an exclusive trade, using hand-printing techniques and printing mostly on long printing tables.

In the 1950s there was a noticeable increase in textile screen printing in the United States and abroad through the development of completely automatic screen-printing machines. While greater speeds are obtainable on these machines, less emphasis is being placed on higher speeds and more emphasis is being placed on the creative spirit and on obtaining styles, designs and color impact not possible with roller-machine printing and other methods. As the principle of technology frees the printer more and more from drudgery, it also requires more knowledge and more creative spirit on his part.

The increase in the use of screen-printing machines and the increasing quality possible with screen printing is causing some roller printers to abandon roller-printing in exchange for screen printing, or at least to supplement textile decorating with screen printing. The large and early established textile screen-printing plants are abandoning hand methods and moving into automatic and semi-automatic textile printing. Firms doing roller printing are also using screen printing for short runs and for printing samples. Large shops employing screen-printing methods can produce up to 20,000 prints of various sizes each day. Machines are not merely replacing hand printing; they are being used for a wide variety of purposes.

There are reasons for this growth. Screen-printing on textile materials is the most versatile of the textile-printing processes just as screen printing is the most flexible of all printing processes. This versatility may become even greater with such new developments as heat-transfer printing involving plastisol and sublimation inks. Quality screen printing done mechanically, semi-automatically and manually is producing such items as high quality drapery materials, decorated silk, wool, linen and synthetic fiber goods, terry-cloth materials, tablecloths, blouses, skirts, bags of all types, ties, window shade materials, smocks, athletic apparel and napkins.

In addition to versatility and the ability to print a variety of items made from different textile materials, there are other advantages to screen-printing on textiles. The size and length of the repeat pattern that can be printed is unlimited in comparison with roller printing or other methods. In roller printing, the size of the pattern is controlled by the size of the roller; printing screens may be made virtually any size. Detail and very large areas may also be printed. Screen printing is practical for blotch printing—a direct printing method in which the background color is uniformly printed rather than dyed. The process achieves exacting color effects at lower costs and offers freedom of artistic expression, since it is more economical for short runs.

Any number of colors may be printed. Because dye inks and dyes are transparent, it is possible to print a varied number of colors by superimposing or overlapping them. For example, the printer can print three colors and obtain six or more, depending on how he overlaps them. Screen printing produces a heavier deposit of ink (or dye) which better penetrates the material. The crushing action of the rollers on the dye in machine-roller printing has a tendency to reduce color bloom; the lack of this type of pressure in screen printing yields more intense and brighter colors. In roller printing, duplex printing (printing on both sides of the material) may be needed to produce decoration on both sides of the fabric; this is often necessary with thicker fabrics. Because of the heavier dye deposit in screen printing, duplex printing may not be necessary. However, duplex printing can be done on vertical screen- printing machines with two screens, clamped and registered exactly, on each side of such materials as blankets, quilts and carpets. Duplex printing may also be accomplished on a duplex rotary screen-printing machine (Patent No. 3,398,680) which will print designs on heavy fabrics such as drapery fabrics and toweling, printing simultaneously on both sides, with the design penetrating through the entire fabric.

The cost of printing screens is low compared to that of engraved printing rollers. Also, the printer may prepare his own printing screens without being forced to wait for outside service. This can be accomplished with the various available direct photographic screen-printing emulsions and films which have been developed by manufacturers and suppliers, in some cases specifically for textile and ceramic screen printing. The photographic printing screens and related photographic processes and materials make it possible to simulate or reproduce any textile-printing method, printing thousands of yards of material from one screen. A shorter time period is required to change a printing screen on a machine than to change printing rollers.

Dyes developed for general textile printing are constantly being adapted to screen printing, and internationally, the dye industry is answering the needs of textile screen printing. Screen-printing manufacturers and suppliers have developed direct dyes since World War II specifically for screen printing: In printing with direct colors it is possible to see the colors as soon as they are printed. There are dye inks (oil-in-water emulsions) which can be applied to cotton, rayon, triacetates, polyamides, polyester, acrylics, glass and other natural and synthetic fibers and blends. These dye prints require two operations—driving off volatile materials by air-drying the printed material, and setting or heat-curing the print to fix the color to the cloth. In addition to dyes, printing screens can also apply flexible lacquers, pigments, adhesives for flocking, resists, rubber cements, plastisol inks, sublimation dyes and other screen-printing-type dyes that do not require complex fixing of the printed cloth.

A modest financial outlay will start one in this field, producing quality printing with manual methods and printing on stationary tables. The simplicity of the operation will permit the expert printer to do this with small financial and labor expenditure. If a mistake is made in hand or semi-automatic printing, it can easily be caught, and unlike in roller printing, there is not much wasted material before the mistake is discovered. Screen printing makes it possible to print more than one thickness of cloth; for example, voile may be printed in layers with a thinner paste color. With the introduction of labor-saving techniques such as the mechanical squeegee and the one-man squeegee (see Figure 5), one operator may print with very large screens and with less fatigue.

All these advantages are made possible by the principle of screen printing which employs a printing screen as a means of applying the dye paste (or color), or screen-printing inks in the form of the design. For the information of the novice (and with apology to the advanced printer), a printing screen generally consists of a frame onto which is stretched a fabric mesh or screen fabric that has open spaces in the areas of the fabric representing the design to be printed. See Figure 6. The rest of the screen

Figure 5. A Cincinnati One-Man Squeegee with a maximum stroke of 48″ x 80″ (122cm x 203cm) and a device for automatically lowering and lifting the printing screen over a vacuum table designed for printing a variety of materials. (Courtesy of Cincinnati Printing & Drying Systems, Inc., Cincinnati, OH)

fabric (which may be polyester, nylon, silk or metal cloth) is filled-in or blocked-out by photographic means, or by hand with a filler. When the dye or ink is pushed or rolled through the open parts, the paste goes through only those parts and deposits itself on the textile material under the screen. Because the various types of dyes and inks used in printing have different solvents in them, different coatings or emulsions are employed for filling-in or blocking-out the desired areas of the screens. Each filler or blockout must resist the dye, the solvent action or the ink being printed.

The stencil is the basis of screen printing. A stencil is a flat sheet of paper, metal or other material out of which design areas have been cut. While it is maintained that the Japanese prepared stencils, and used human hair to hold the main design circles and other details to prevent them from falling out, modern screen printing, using mesh fabric, developed in the United States during the first decade of the twentieth century.

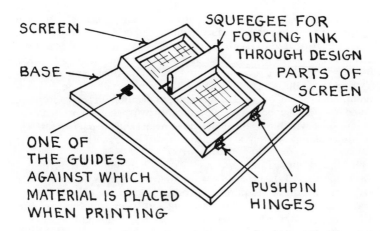

SCREEN

BASE

SQUEEGEE FOR
FORCING INK
THROUGH DESIGN
PARTS OF
SCREEN

ONE OF
THE GUIDES
AGAINST WHICH
MATERIAL IS PLACED
WHEN PRINTING

PUSHPIN
HINGES

Figure 6. **A simple screen-printing unit showing the principle of screen printing.**

During the printing operation, the screen may be carried manually and placed on the material, or the fabric may be placed or moved under the screen during the printing operation. In the case of the rotary screen-printing machine, the material moves around the circular or curved printing screen. For printing purposes, dyestuff solutions (dispersions) are thickened to form a paste with similar viscosity to that of screen-printing inks used for general screen printing. The printing pastes are manufactured in various viscosities so that pastes are avaiable with low, medium or high solid content. If a screen-printing dye or ink is to be thinned or changed in any fashion, the manufacturer's directions will specify the exact manner in which this should be done.

Because there is no one universal procedure used to print on textiles, usually the fabric or material to be printed must first be identified and its end use known. The end use of the product often governs the printing process. If there is any doubt about the composition of the fabric, or if the printer is unsure what fibers the cloth may contain, he can get help from the dye manufacturer, mills or from the source where the material was purchased. There are also simple tests for determining fabric type.

If the material is not ready for printing, it should be prepared by washing to remove sizing, fillers and impurities, in order for the dye to better penetrate the cloth. While there are other methods of preparing cloth for printing, such as singeing, destarching, treating with alkali or acid and bleaching, in general, printers may just concern themselves with washing the material. With many jobs, this may not be necessary.

15

It depends on the use of the fabric. After the design is chosen, the printing screens prepared and the fabric printed and dried, the fabric is heat-cured or heat-treated to fix the dye or make the print fast so that it will resist washing, dry-cleaning, wet and dry crocking and other effects. *Crocking* is the degree to which a dyed print or printed cloth will mark-off or wear off due to friction. Often the printer will not be involved in complex heat treatment. For example, in printing on terry-cloth, the printed material may be dried and heat-cured by placing the printed items on conveyors which pass through heated ovens and are packed for shipping immediately as they are removed from the oven.

The "hand" or stiffness which may remain in the material from the printing paste will disappear after the first washing by the purchaser. Some pigments do not require heat-curing to make the print fast; some dyes and pigments will require steaming and special equipment. After the heat treatment, the material is rinsed well in water to remove thickening, surplus dyes and chemicals. It must be stressed that getting the best results in textile screen printing is dependent on the exact handling of each of the above interdependent steps of the total printing operation, on experimentation and on following the instructions of the dye or ink manufacturer when using colors, inks and additives. After the printer has done some printing, he may start to modify formulations. However, these modifications must be based on complete and objective test results made under local shop conditions to determine the best printing paste formulations for the job, and on the end results required.

Electrostatic Screen Printing

Electrically heated metal mesh screens have been and are being used to print thermoplastic ceramic inks onto glassware and ceramic ware. However, the principle of this type of printing differs from that of electrostatic screen printing.

Electrostatic screen printing employs the principle of controlling static electricity in order to form a printed design or visible image. This type of printing has been used for printing on textiles and wallpaper. The invention of the principle, by Clyde O. Childress and Louis J. Kabell of the United States, was announced in 1961 by the Stanford Research Institute. This process employs an electrically charged conducting screen (or printing screen), which acts as the design-forming master. It has the potential to produce exact prints on irregularly-shaped surfaces such as potato chips, cheesecloth, hot metals, avocados, hot glass, live animals, corrugated boards and foam rubber. It produces designs, illustrations and images on flat and complex surfaces without the normal contact of an image-carrying printing plate, eliminating the need for pressure and uniformity of contact.

The printing involves an electrically charged master (a mesh screen) and a conducting backing plate or electric ground placed in a parallel position to the screen. The preparation of the master printing screen is done in a similar fashion to that of a direct-coated synthetic emulsion screen. Printing is done with the application of a special type of "electroscopic" ink on the inside (squeegee side) of the screen. The ink consists of finely-ground, spherically-shaped particles made up of an appropriate resin and a coloring matter. Generally, electroscopic inks have no solvent and are made up of dyed ink particles or of thermoadhesive pigment resins such as styrene, copolymers, polyamides, ethyl cellulose or natural resins such as rosin or gum.

The ink takes the electrical charge from the screen and is attracted through the openings toward the grounding back plate. The openings in the screen, of course, represent the design areas to be printed. The ink travels straight through, sticks to the back of the plate and reproduces a faithful pattern of the image in the openings of the screen. Any material, article or substance which is placed between the two plates will be printed, and the image can then be fixed by the application of heat, solvent or other means, depending on the ink used. The electrical charge is obtained by applying a voltage between the printing screen and the conductive plate. The intercepting article can be anything which does not interfere with the electrical field, anything that is not electrically charged.

This process can print detail and large-area printing; multicolor work may be done by using a different screen for each color. One screen may print as many as 100,000 impressions. The printer should be cognizant of the process, not only for textile printing, but for other types of printing to supplement regular screen printing.

In summary, while textile screen printing is a specialized field, it can be learned by the printer and the novice. Even though the general printer is doing some textile printing daily with direct pigment dyes and oil-vehicle inks, he will have to carefully standardize each of his steps in the total textile-printing procedure when working with chemical dyes and pigments. He must be on the alert for, but not dwarfed by, the constant impact of the new, interesting experiences and knowledge he will have to gain. He should keep an objective record of all his printing experiences that pertain to color mixing, formulations, variations in formulations, heat-curing time and temperature, drying of printed matter, the various materials that can be printed with one given dye ink and sources for obtaining dyes and inks. The printer who is seriously planning to do textile screen printing can receive technical help from his screen-printing supplier, dye and ink manufacturer, equipment manufacturer and from the textile mills and firms selling fabrics to him. His records based on experience, and the available technical assistance from the above sources, will very quickly fill the void originally created by his lack of specialized knowledge.

Figure 7 presents a multicolored bolt material, precision screen-printed on a completely automatic machine.

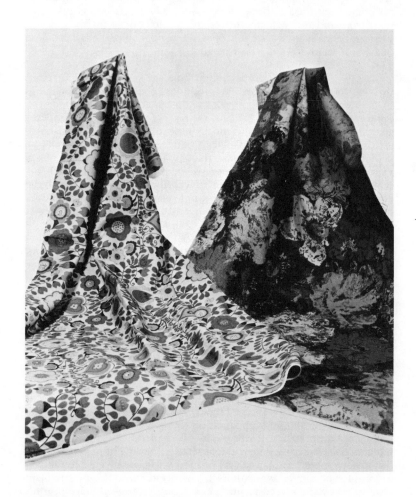

Figure 7. A nine-color cotton drapery material that was screen-printed on a machine that carries out all printing operations automatically, allowing the printed material to enter a drying unit where it is thoroughly dried and rolled up for further processing. (Courtesy of Northern Dyeing Corp., and Castle Creek Prints, Inc., Washington, NJ)

18

Chapter III

UNITS FOR SCREEN PRINTING ON TEXTILE SURFACES

First ventures by printers in screen-printing on textiles usually begin with a modest financial outlay, and include printing one-piece items. Few printers start textile screen printing by decorating yard goods with costly equipment. As the printer advances in his techniques and increases his clientele, he will ultimately mechanize or at least produce printing semi-automatically.

Single-piece textile items may be printed on simple screen-printing units. Ordinary screen-printing units which use small and large screens, special hand-printing set-ups, (illustrated in Figures 8 through 15), long printing tables and specially designed and built screen-printing textile machines, are used to print with the varied screen-printing inks and dyes on different textile surfaces. The printer may build these units or purchase them from screen-printing suppliers. Figure 8 shows a one-screen printing unit, used in England, which may be attached to a small printing table (or base) or to the end of a long textile-printing table. This screen will save time when printing the same design on two single items which are registered in the required spots on the table. The multi-screen printing table shown in Figure 9 may be used for printing up to three colors with medium and large-size screens on terry-cloth, denim, plastic, sign cloth, cotton and impregnated cloth. The processor may also attach a wooden prop bar to the screen frame to keep the screens in a raised position on the multi-screen unit. The squeegees should have nails driven in at the ends of the handles so that the nails extend past the trough and prevent the squeegee from falling into the dye or ink.

The hand-printing set-up presented in Figure 10 shows a unit which the writer has used for printing on bolt material; it may also be used for decorating wallpaper, vinyl material, oil-cloth and window shade material. While this unit does not produce great printing speeds, ver-

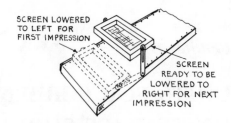

SCREEN LOWERED
TO LEFT FOR
FIRST IMPRESSION

SCREEN
READY TO BE
LOWERED TO
RIGHT FOR NEXT
IMPRESSION

Figure 8. **A single screen two-impression unit that may be fastened to a printing base or to a table covered with padding, for textile-printing two individual items.**

satility of work and the application of more than one color may be accomplished. Any size screen may be attached to this unit by fastening it to the master frame. Printing screens may be attached to the master frame with strips of wood or metal which may be fastened to the top of the screen and the master frame. Also, the master frame may be counterbalanced to keep the screen automatically in a raised position. The base (or table) for the screen should be prepared and padded the same way as long textile screen-printing tables. The festooner or rod arrangement employed for drying and airing the printed material can be built so that the rods hang from the ceiling, leaving more floor space for other uses. The printed fabric is pulled over the rods or festooner so that the unprinted side of the fabric comes in contact with the rods, preventing "mark-off" (rubbing off of the dye) on the rods or on the material itself. Instead of building the printing table, the printer may also use a modern one-man squeegee unit with the festooner arrangement to obtain the same results.

The transparent registration flap (illustrated in Figures 9 and 10) is a practical aid for registering more than one color of dye or ink on irregularly-shaped materials and on textile materials which are too flexible to be registered against guides. The registration flap eliminates the necessity of inserting solid forms in such items as sports shirts and gloves in order to print them. The flap may be a sheet of transparent or translucent plastic or strong tracing paper which is tacked or taped as shown in the illustrations. In registering the material to be printed, the design is printed in the first color on the registration flap. The material to be printed is placed under the print on the transparent sheet, and the registration sheet is folded out of the way. The material to be printed is left in the exact spot in which it was placed and the printing screen in brought down over the correctly registered material and printed in the usual manner. This procedure of placing the piece to be printed under the print on the registration flap, folding the flap out of the way, and printing, is repeated for each impression and for each color. However, once the registration print is made on the flap, the placing and printing of the irregularly shaped object or material becomes a simple procedure.

Printing tables used for hand textile screen printing and for semi-automatic printing are similar to those originally employed for hand block printing, except that the screen-printing tables must be long enough to accommodate the longest bolts of fabrics and other materials that the

20

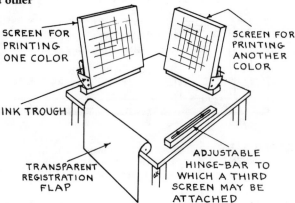

Figure 9. A multicolor screen-printing unit used for hand-printing on textile materials and other products.

SCREEN FOR
PRINTING
ONE COLOR

SCREEN FOR
PRINTING
ANOTHER
COLOR

INK TROUGH

TRANSPARENT
REGISTRATION
FLAP

ADJUSTABLE
HINGE-BAR TO
WHICH A THIRD
SCREEN MAY BE
ATTACHED

Figure 10. A hand-printing unit used for screen-printing on fabrics, wallpaper and rug material.

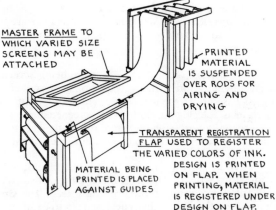

MASTER FRAME TO
WHICH VARIED SIZE
SCREENS MAY BE
ATTACHED

PRINTED
MATERIAL
IS SUSPENDED
OVER RODS FOR
AIRING AND
DRYING

TRANSPARENT REGISTRATION
FLAP USED TO REGISTER
THE VARIED COLORS OF INK.
DESIGN IS PRINTED
ON FLAP. WHEN
PRINTING, MATERIAL
IS REGISTERED UNDER
DESIGN ON FLAP.

MATERIAL BEING
PRINTED IS PLACED
AGAINST GUIDES

printer will be printing. In spite of automation fever, these long tables with portable printing screens and hand or semi-automatic squeegeeing are still employed because quality work can be done on them in small and large plants with less expenditure than the investment required for automated screen printing. The tables (see Figures 11, 13 and 14) are six or more feet in width and about 30 inches in height, so that the table is not too high or inconvenient for printing. The printing table should be about twelve inches wider than the largest screen normally used in the shop. The top of the table is uniformly flat and even. Pressed board,

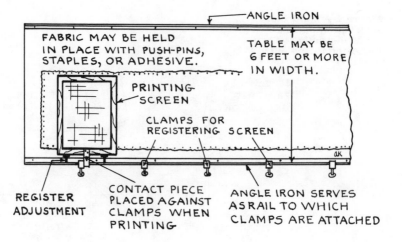

ANGLE IRON

FABRIC MAY BE HELD
IN PLACE WITH PUSH-PINS,
STAPLES, OR ADHESIVE.

TABLE MAY BE
6 FEET OR MORE
IN WIDTH.

PRINTING-
SCREEN

CLAMPS FOR
REGISTERING SCREEN

REGISTER
ADJUSTMENT

CONTACT PIECE
PLACED AGAINST
CLAMPS WHEN
PRINTING

ANGLE IRON SERVES
AS RAIL TO WHICH
CLAMPS ARE ATTACHED

Figure 11. **A top view of a textile screen-printing table showing the various parts of this hand-printing unit.**

wood panels, asbestos sheets and concrete have been used as materials for the tops of tables. While most of the tables are built perfectly flat and level, some have tops that are slanted at an angle to make manual squeegeeing easier.

When thicker or heavier fabrics are being screen printed, making perfect penetration difficult to obtain, some screen printers have used a glass base under the screen, screening one impression of dye or ink on the glass, placing the cloth on the screened impression, and then printing a second impression on top of the cloth. This technique helps produce penetration of the color on both sides of the cloth.

As can be seen in Figures 11, 13 and 14, one side of the table has a rail with a series of adjustable metal clamps or stops fastened at desired intervals for registering the printing screen. The size of each interval depends on the size of the repeat pattern to be printed, and on the size of the printing screen. The screen also has an adjustable contact piece and a registration mechanism or machine bolts to ensure that the pattern will be printed in the exact desired spot on the fabric. The bolts allow the screen to be registered by turning them in or out, depending on whether the processor desires to move the screen away from the rail or toward the rail.

When printing, the screen is lifted and placed against the clamps (guides). One or both sides of the table may be used, using one or two operators on each side and printing an impression at every other stop.

Figure 12. A hinge designed for the quick clamping of any size screen for printing: The hinges may be fastened to the printing base or to the table. (Courtesy of Naz-Dar Co., Chicago, IL)

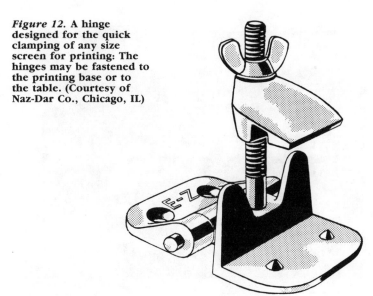

Figure 13. A method of registering the screen for printing repeat patterns on textile screen-printing tables.

SCREEN

ADJUSTABLE
CONTACT
PIECE

RAIL

SCREWS OR
BOLTS FASTENED
TO SCREEN FRAME
ARE USED TO REGISTER
SCREEN. TURNING
SCREWS OUT OR IN
MOVES SCREEN AWAY
FROM RAIL OR TOWARD RAIL.

C-CLAMPS SERVE AS
GUIDES AGAINST WHICH
CONTACT PIECE RESTS
DURING PRINTING OPERATION.

For example, the operator may first print only the odd-numbered stops. When he reaches the end of the table, he may then start at the beginning again and print the even-numbered stops. The design and the color printed will govern whether the printer should print one stop after another or skip stops. Sometimes a third operator will be used to hold the large screen in place while two individuals do the squeegeeing manually. However, the printer must make sure that the design is first registered carefully on the fabric so that the printing is done in exactly the same position for each repeat color pattern. The printing may be done "wet on wet," meaning that the screen is placed on the previously printed damp color. When very large screens are used for printing, two operators are used. However, with the available one-arm squeegee ar-

Figure 14. **Students doing manual screen-printing on drapery material. (Courtesy of The American Crayon Company, Sandusky, OH)**

rangements, it is possible for one operator to use large screens with less fatigue than when using a hand squeegee.

Figure 15 presents a hand textile-decorating unit used for printing repeat patterns with small screens on large pieces of fabric. This method of registering (placing) the screen for printing may be used on large and small printing tables.

Textile printing has paid considerable attention to squeegees, since the squeegee plays an important role in transferring the dye or ink to the fabric. In addition to the wide use of rubber for the squeegee blade, squeegees made of straight-grained lightweight wood, pneumatic squeegees, dye-impregnated felt and squeegees with glass rods are sometimes used to apply dye and dye inks. Generally, a soft squeegee is used on a soft surface and a harder squeegee on a hard surface. Also, soft, dull squeegees deposit more color; sharp squeegees deposit less color. Thus, for hand textile-printing, the squeegee blade should be somewhat rounded. For machine printing, the shape of the squeegee blade is usually recommended by the manufacturer. The angle of the squeegee to the screen influences color penetration and evenness in printing. Expert printers recommend that the squeegee be positioned or held at an angle of twenty to 45 degrees for the most practical application of the dye.

24

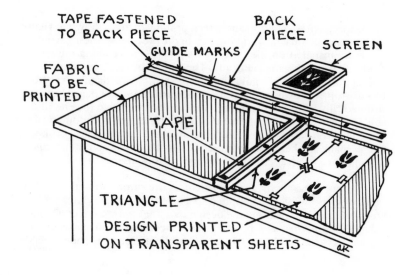

TAPE FASTENED TO BACK PIECE

BACK PIECE

GUIDE MARKS

SCREEN

FABRIC TO BE PRINTED

TAPE

TRIANGLE

DESIGN PRINTED ON TRANSPARENT SHEETS

Figure 15. Printing a repeat pattern with a small screen on a large piece of fabric.

This technique of printing, recommended by The American Crayon Co., Sandusky, OH, uses a right triangle and a back piece fastened along the length of the table as register guides.

The triangle and the back piece are made of lumber. The triangle should be made of hard wood that is of sufficient weight to prevent the frame from moving during printing, and should fit the printing area. It may be finished with a coat of lacquer or varnish.

Masking tape or gummed paper tape is taped on top of the back piece and on the triangle. The tape may be fastened vertically on the side of the back piece and the triangle rather than horizontally.

1. Make enough proofs of the design on thin transparent paper to cover the width of the cloth to be printed. Tape the proofs together.

2. Place the proofs on the fabric, and place the triangle against the proofs.

3. Now register the dry screen over the first proof, placing the screen against the back piece and against the triangle.

4. Make guide marks (with crayon or pencil) that correspond to the screen frame edges, on the back piece tape and on the triangle tape.

5. Finish making guide marks for the rest of the width of the screen on the back piece and for the length of the screen on the triangle.

6. Printing is done by placing the triangle against the back piece, then placing the screen against the guide marks on the triangle and on the back piece.

25

Felt impregnated with dye can also be used to apply the color. This is accomplished by placing the screen over the fabric, placing the felt over the screen and applying pressure over the felt with a roller (or brayer).

The mechanized or automatic screen-printing carriage shown in Figure 16 eliminates manual labor on the part of the processor. These carriages, which are installed on the long printing table, move along the length of the table, printing mechanically. The automatic carriage is supported by a supporting rail and a guide rail. As the printing carriage moves from stop to stop, the printing screen on the carriage is raised and lowered automatically, printing the desired repeat pattern. When the end of the table is reached, the carriage returns to its starting point automatically. The unit can be adjusted so that it prints with one squeegee stroke or with as many strokes as are required for good penetration of the color. The squeegee or scraper in the carriage is easily inserted and removed.

From one to as many as twenty colors are printed on tables. Also, the writer has on occasion applied special effects by spraying an ink or dye color and then printing the design over the sprayed effect. Opaque and metallic inks may also be sprayed over textile-printed materials. Different effects can be obtained by using different squeegees and squeegee blades.

A cushioning effect is needed when printing on tables to prevent the dye paste from producing irregular prints and from smudging. The printed fabric is held semi-permanently on top of the cushioning layer. The layer for hand-printing tables consists of felt that is about 3/16″ thick and in contact with the table; a sheet of waterproof fabric, oilcloth, polyethylene or a plastic cover is stretched over the felt layer; and a "back grey" cloth is stretched over the waterproof layer. The waterproof layer

Figure 16. **An automatic carriage used for screen-printing on textile tables. (Courtesy of Societe Alsacienne de Constructions Mecaniques, Cambridge, MA)**

26

prevents the dye paste from penetrating the felt. The back grey cloth, a cotton fabric material, is placed below and next to the fabric being printed. Its purpose is to absorb the dye paste that may penetrate and smudge the fabric being printed. The back grey may be washed and used over and over. It receives its name from the cloth that is used in machine roller printing and is the layer between the fabric being printed and the blanket around the roller. The layers on the table must be stretched in such a way that a smooth, taut surface is obtained for printing.

It is essential that the fabric to be printed is fastened to the table so that it is stationary and does not move under the action of the squeegee or automatic carriage. The beginner usually pins or staples his fabric over the grey cloth. However, as the dye penetrates the fabric it has a tendency to contract and distort the material. For this reason, adhesives and gums have come to be used to hold the fabric to the table or to the back grey or to the conveyor blankets on screen-printing machines during printing. Very sheer materials may be pinned to the back grey, because adhesives may migrate or work through the material being printed. The adhesives available are generally of a semi-permanent nature and are of the water-soluble type, synthetic-resin type, or of the rubber-base solvent type. The adhesive or gum may be applied at the edges or under the entire fabric being printed. In some cases, before applying the rubber-type adhesive over the back grey, a pre-sizing of starch on the back grey is recommended.

The table coatings or adhesives may be applied by brushing or squeegeeing them directly onto the table surface or the fabric being printed. Generally, good adhesives will not transfer to the material being printed, and will hold up under many impressions. Although there are pressure-sensitive adhesives which are manufactured specifically for textile screen printing, care must be used in selecting the proper type and in applying the minimum necessary to hold the material and to ensure that the adhesive does not prevent even absorption of the color.

The adhesive is easy to apply, may be diluted with water or a solvent recommended by the supplier, and is fast drying. Several coats may be needed to obtain an adhesive surface, allowing each coat to dry thoroughly. The material to be printed is pressed gently over the adhesive. There are semi-permanent adhesives that do not absorb water-soluble printing dyes, and when the printed cloth is removed, the table may be washed. When the adhesive on the table is dry, another layer of fabric may be pressed down without regumming or applying another coat of adhesive. With some adhesives this may be done more than a dozen times without further application of adhesive.

Another way of attaching the fabric for printing is to adhere it over the back grey cloth with a combining machine. Then the combined fabric and back grey are rolled down the table and fastened at the edges of the back grey with hooks or with adhesive at the sides of the table. After printing, the material is removed, the back grey washed, and another combined roll of cloth and back grey is rolled down, eliminating the need to wash the table.

There are gumming or pasting machines designed especially to apply adhesives or gums to the printing table in any thickness. At the same time the adhesive is being coated onto the table, the fabric to be printed is rolled firmly over the adhesive. After printing, the adhesive may be removed from the table or from the back grey cloth with warm water and detergent, with toluene, methyl ethyl ketone and toulol or ethyl acetate, depending on the type of table adhesive used.

Thus, to print effectively on fabric, the fabric must first be held, secured or pasted down correctly, printed and then stripped from the table for further processing, again depending on the type of dye used.

Figure 16A shows a textile screen-printing machine, that is available in eight to twelve stations for automatic printing in accurate register on flexible or rigid material with standard inks or dyes. The machine will print eight different colors in perfect register on a substrate, or will print the same design wet, and will print more than eight colors by superimposing transparent colors one on top of another. Each printing unit can be controlled from each individual station or from one "command" station. The fabric or garment is loaded on a special platen or base and is accurately and automatically registered at each printing station.

Figure 16A. An "Arrow Multiprinter" Automatic Screen-Printing Machine that is designed to print up to eight colors, and prints design areas up to 16″ x 14″ (35.56cm x 20.46cm) on garments, jackets, T-shirts, bags, bowling shirts, cut pieces and aprons. Each of the eight print heads operates independently with its own set of controls. With flash-cure units inserted into the print heads following each color station, it is possible to run four-color process jobs, flash-curing each color before printing the next one. (Courtesy of Advance Process Supply Co., Chicago, IL)

28

Chapter IV

SCREEN-PRINTING TEXTILE MACHINES

While textile products were being printed on semi-automatic screen-printing units and on some screen-printing presses before 1940, automatic textile and garment screen printing began with the end of World War II. The construction of automated machines started in 1944 and machines were available commercially in 1948. Different machines for automated textile screen printing developed in various parts of the world (See Figures 17 to 27H).

Although originally some screen printers were forced to build their own machines and mechanical units, today textile units for garment and screen printing are being designed and built by specialists.

The growing market for screen printing developed because of its emphasis on better styling and design. The process offered more artistic expression to textile designers for smaller runs than was possible with machine roller printing. Other factors which helped the growth of machine textile screen printing were the availability of screen-printing color pastes and dyes, the availability of screen-printing emulsions and films for the preparation of printing screens, the lesser financial investment required for the installation of mechanical screen printing compared with machine roller printing, the lesser cost and easier preparation of printing screens and the fact that labor could be easily trained. A very important influence in the use of textile printing machinery in screen-printing shops in the early 1970s was the impact of textile transfer printing.

Screen-printing machines have no restriction on the size or length of the repeat pattern or the number of colors printed. Also, the printing of such items as towels, throw rugs with pile and bath mats may be accomplished. The machines are easy to operate, and the average repeat

Figure 17. Below. The Precision Midas Textile Printing Machine (showing feed-end) introduced the "flood stroke" to the textile industry. The machine prints repeats varying from 28 inches (71cm) to 120 inches (305cm) per repeat pattern; the longer the repeat, the greater the yardage per hour. The production rate may be 1800 yards (1645.92m) per hour for the 120-inch repeats. (Courtesy of Precision Screen Machines, Inc., Hawthorne, NJ and Pageland Screen Printers, Pageland, SC)

Figure 18. Above. Another view of a Precision Textile Printing Machine that is 130 feet (39.6m) long with a 72-inch (183cm) wide blanket. The machine will print six colors on a 120″ (305cm) repeat; twelve colors on a 60″ (152cm) repeat; and fifteen colors on a 40″ (102cm) repeat. (Courtesy of Precision Screen Machines, Inc., Hawthorne, NJ and Printed Fabrics, Inc., Carrollton, GA)

Figure 19. The Buser Screen-Printing Machine, illustrating a feed-in unit at the front and a drying unit at the far end, is about 130 feet (39.62m) long, prints up to ten colors, and can handle 48-inch (121.92cm) repeats and a maximum printing width of up to 66 inches (167.64cm).

Figure 20. The feed-in unit and the thermoplastic gluing system on the Buser screen-print machine. (Courtesy of Jungfrau, Inc., Cedar Grove, NJ)

size or pattern on the machines ranges from twenty to 130 inches and allows up to sixteen colors to be printed.

At first, the low rate of production of screen printing limited the yardage of a design and gave the printing an exclusive value which it still has. Not only large screen-printing shops began to use automatic screen machines, but roller machine printers began to employ the process to supplement their machine printing which is generally governed by a fixed machine design and does not have the color bloom produced by screen-printing machines. Screen-printing machines can be designed or altered to suit individual textile plant needs. Some machines are manufactured from standard parts and components that are available from better suppliers of machine parts or hardware suppliers, which allows for easy replacement of parts. All these advantages emphasized the fact that printing is a method of decorating fabrics, and that screen printing produced decorating advantages. The machines are being changed and improved constantly to answer the needs of the screen-printing and textile-printing industries. It must be emphasized that while hand screen-printing on textiles produces accurate register (accuracy in printing) in the desired spot each time on the fabric for multicolor work, the perseverance of engineering and screen-printing talents achieved high speed and precise textile screen printing which often surpasses hand textile printing.

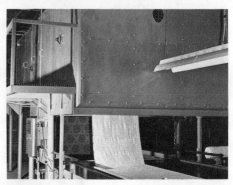

Figure 21. **Printed goods leaving the print machine and going into the drying unit. The printed material is peeled away from the conveyor belt as the material feeds vertically into the dryer. (Courtesy of Jungfrau, Inc., Cedar Grove, NJ)**

The textile screen-printing machine uses an endless conveyor as a blanket, often faced with or impregnated with synthetic rubber, onto which the textile material to be printed is adhered semi-permanently, combined with, or placed and usually synchronized with, a drying unit. The principle of machine textile screen printing (both on flat and rotary-type machines) generally consists of a machine with a device such as a blanket upon which the cloth to be printed is fed to the printing screen which may be flat or round in shape, the screen-printing unit, and a dryer into which the printed cloth is fed to dry or heat-cure and set the colors (See Figures 21 and 25). The cloth is fed under the correct tension which

Figure 22. **The Zimmer Automatic Printing Machine illustrating the printing of two widths of cloth with different patterns, each pattern being 49 1/4 inches (125cm) in size. The machine employs a steel roller which is controlled magnetically and produces sharp and detailed prints. (Courtesy of Societe Alsacienne de Constructions Mecaniques, Cambridge, MA)**

32

Figure 23. The Rice Barton-Meccanotessile Automatic Screen-Printing Machine which was designed to print on any lightweight or thick fabric, is available in eight to sixteen color units and in 63″ or 75″ (160cm or 190.5cm) standard printing widths. The machine has an endless blanket, an automatic blanket cleaning unit and a dryer synchronized with the machine printing speed. The printed fabric is run through the dryer from one to nine times without the risk of smearing. (Courtesy of Rice Barton Corp., Worcester, MA)

Figure 24. The squeegee units on the Rice Barton-Meccanotessile machine allow for the use of any screen in the carrier and for screen adjustment in all directions, thus making off-contact printing possible. Each unit may be started or stopped independently and allows for the use of varied types of squeegee blades for different types of printing. (Courtesy of Rice Barton Corp., Worcester, MA)

Figure 25. A modern Precision Screen printing machine used for printing on towels and cut parts. (Courtesy of Precision Screen Machines, Hawthorne, NJ)

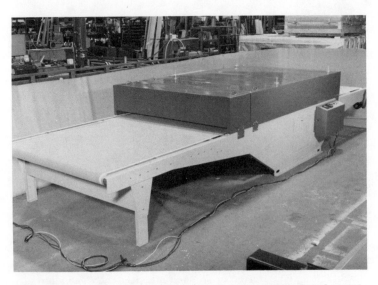

Figure 26. A gas-fired dryer used for drying textile-printed parts. (Courtesy of Precision Screen Machines, Hawthorne, NJ)

is automatically maintained to prevent the formation of creases under the printing screen.

The blankets usually are resistant to wear, printing pastes, pigments and the solvents employed for screen-process dye printing. Uniform films of adhesive, gum, paste or glue are applied automatically over the blanket as the cloth to be printed is combined with the conveyor blanket. The deposit of the adhesive may be varied to suit different fabrics. Various methods are employed to stabilize blanket movement and the starting and stopping of the blanket. After printing, the blankets are washed automatically with a blanket-washing device which is adapted to work with the printing speeds of the machine. As the washed blanket enters the entry side of the machine, a gluing device again coats a film of adhesive onto the blanket for combining with the cloth to be printed. Figure 20 illustrates a thermoplastic gluing system. Thermoplastic materials soften when heat is applied to them, and harden upon cooling. The gluing system shown consists of a heating plate which presses the cloth to be printed down on the conveyor belt; the conveyor belt has been pre-treated with a thermoplastic adhesive that is not water-soluble.

Generally, screen-printing textile machines are of two types—the flat-bed machine and the rotary screen-printing machine. The flat-bed machine uses flat printing screens, usually arranged horizontally, one after the other, with the cloth passing on a continuous belt under the flat screens, one screen printing its color after the other (see Figures 22 and 24). The blanket travel is pre-set on the machines so that the cloth moves the exact distance to the register or indexes, and a repeat pattern is printed. As the conveyor advances, either by hydraulic, magnetic or mechanical means (depending on the machine), the length of the repeat pattern is advanced to the printing position. The printing screen is then lowered, the squeegee moves across to deposit dye paste onto the cloth, and the screen is raised again to begin another printing cycle. The conveyor belt and the fabric are held securely to ensure an accurate register of colors. After the fabric is printed, it is passed through a hot-air dryer unit and then to a coiling unit for the further processing of the cloth should it be necessary.

The rotary screen-printing machine has cylindrically round screens which are usually made of thin perforated metal. The perforations and thickness of the metal may vary, depending on the type of fabric and the design to be printed. The cloth on the rotary machine is automatically fixed onto a continuous belt or printing blanket. The cylinder screens are fitted into stands on both sides of the blanket. The cloth on the blanket is printed as the blanket passes under or around the screen, the screens and the blanket moving at the same speed. Printing speeds are higher on the rotary screen-printing machine. After printing, the cloth is fed into a dryer.

Rotary machines make it possible to print continuous longitudinal stripes, large blotches, imitations of gradual color shading and pinpoint effects. The rotary screen may be set into the machine so that the screen prints either warpwise or weftwise. Printing warpwise means printing with the length of the fabric, or parallel to the selvage; weftwise means printing across, or perpendicular to the length of the cloth. The selvage is the edge of the woven fabric that is finished to prevent unraveling. Figures 27H and 27G illustrate two types of rotary screen-printing machines.

Figure 27. Profiles or cross sections of squeegees on some screen-printing textile machines: A. Buser Hydromag; B. Reggiani Meccanofilm; C. Comerio Ercole Screen Printing Machine; D. Stork; E. Zimmer Screen Printing Automat; F. Thorne.

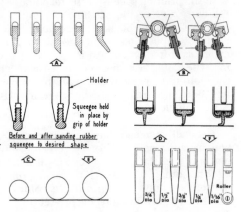

The squeegee used for machine-printing is a very important part of the machine. Unlike the squeegee employed for hand-printing, the shape, material and design of the machine squeegee varies (see Figure 27). In addition to rubber, metal alloys, stainless steel and roller squeegees are used for the blade. Rubber squeegees vary in cross section and hardness. The squeegee can usually be adjusted on each individual screen for correct angle, pressure and number of strokes. In one type of machine the blade may be adjusted so that the rubber will bend at a greater angle, allowing more color to be applied in this specific machine. In this squeegee, the liquid pressure built up in the printing paste can be made to exceed the force exerted on the screen. On some machines, two squeegees, pressing one after the other and placed parallel to one another, are used. Printing with the squeegees is based on the principle of: (1) a hard squeegee printing on a hard surface; (2) a hard squeegee printing on a soft surface; and (3) a soft squeegee working on a hard surface. In machine screen printing there is more uniformity of squeegee pressure than with hand printing, where there may be a difference in pressure as the squeegee passes from one operator to another when the squeegee

36

Figure 27G. A Stork rotary screen-printing machine designed to print up to twenty colors on varied textile materials and on textile transfer paper, printing repeat patterns varying in size from 25.6″ to 73.12″ (640mm to 1928mm), at printing speeds varying from 13.2 to 264 feet (4m to 80m) per minute and printing on material that is up to 128″ (3200mm) wide. (Courtesy of Stork Brabant, Boxmeer, Holland)

Figure 27H. A Precision textile rotary screen-printing machine designed to print up to twelve colors on continuous web printing, printing repeats up to 40 inches (102cm) in size on material that is up to 120 inches (305cm) wide. (Courtesy of Precision Screen Machines, Inc., Hawthorne, NJ)

reaches the middle of the printing table. The machines are made so that the squeegees can be easily inserted and removed when necessary.

Squeegees in rotary screens are precision-fitted inside the cylinder to force the dye or ink through the screen mesh or perforations onto the cloth that is adhered to the blanket. The squeegee is adjustable, and the adjustment may be read on a graduated scale. The squeegee exerts pressure only when contact is made between the screen and the blanket in order to prevent damage to the rotary screen.

The yardage printed per hour is governed not only by the speed of the machine, but by the size of the repeat pattern being printed and by the number of squeegee strokes required for the particular operation. The advantage of short repeat patterns, common to roller printing, is made possible in screen printing by "ganging up" or putting more than one repeat pattern on one printing screen. The "flood stroke" (see Figure 17) is another way of allowing for more speed in the printing process. The flood stroke is used in screen printing for point-of-purchase printing and other general screen printing. In this stroke, as exemplified on the machine illustrated in Figure 17, the squeegee prints in the same direction each time and carries the dye paste in front of itself during the printing cycle. The dye paste is flooded onto the screen with a device attached in front of the squeegee while the screen is in a raised position and while the fabric is moving into the printing position. The flooding mechanism allows the color to be evenly spread over the screen on its return to the starting position of the cycle. The paste is squeegeed onto the fabric with a single stroke. Flooding the screen while it is in a raised position may prevent the need for more than one printing stroke of the squeegee.

In most machines the printing is done "wet on wet." After the fabric has been printed with the first color, it is guided under the screens to the next screen to receive the next color, etc. Machines allow high production with limited labor. Generally, two operators are required. Machines are automated to the point where the machine requires operators only for set-up and for inspection. Inspection in automated printing is very important, because much fabric waste may result if discrepancies are not detected immediately. Although screen-printing textile machines are more expensive than other screen-printing machines, the large textile-printing shops have started using them to meet high production without giving up quality printing.

In summary, today the beginning textile or garment printer has his choice of equipment that may be purchased or built himself, as illustrated in Figures 9, 10, 11, 13, 15 and 65. Also, manual and semi-automatic units for the beginner are available from reliable textile screen-printing dealers.

It must be stressed that textile and garment printing has passed out of the trial and error period and is emerging into a period of constant research, development and refinement which offers greater potential to textile screen printing and to general screen printing.

Chapter V

TEXTILE-TYPE INKS FOR
TEXTILE SCREEN PRINTING

As far as screen-printing inks or dyes are concerned, textile materials have been decorated with the following types: water-based, air-based, oil-based, water-in-oil emulsions, dye-type inks, plastisols, nylon inks and specially developed inks such as glitter, fluorescent, phosphorescent, sublimation-types and puff inks which may be water-based or plastisol-types. All textile inks, except plastisols, must dry before they can be cured or exposed to heat of the correct temperature and time length. When heat is applied in curing (which may vary from about 275 to 300 degrees Fahrenheit), the ink may go through a chemical reaction known as polymerization. Some solvent phase inks can be air-dried, but only if the directions recommend it. However, the average T-shirt printer may come in contact with three basic inks—plastisols, water-based and emulsions. Although, in the printing of any ink, the screen printer must follow the instructions of the ink manufacturer.

The screen-printing of imaginative and attractive designs with dye pastes and inks on various textile materials is a form of localized dyeing. The areas which are printed on the cloth should withstand the same tests of fastness and color resistance to bleaching, perspiration, rubbing, washing and dry cleaning as the cloth which is dyed. Modern textile screen-printing with dyes is a chemical process which combines the dye paste, consisting of specially prepared and formulated chemicals, with the fabrics printed on, so that the printed areas resist removal.

Inks are composed of the following general ingredients: (1) a **colorant** which may consist of pigments or dyes; (2) a **vehicle**—the liquid state of the ink ingredients which makes the ink printable, and which acts as the carrier; (3) a **solvent** which dissolves the solid parts; and (4) **additives** such as reducers, extenders, retarders and catalysts for varying some properties.

40

It should be obvious that the production of an ink formulation is the result of much research and experimentation with chemical ingredients to ensure that the ink will bind itself to varied substrates.

The garment which has been printed with the correct textile ink is expected to dry so that the ink is not wet to the touch. While for some inks drying may also serve as curing, **curing** an ink refers to a special reaction in which heat is used to produce a reaction known as a polymerization, in which small molecules form larger molecules of the same substance.

The type of dye ink used for textile screen printing depends on the particular fabric to be printed, the type of color being applied, the equipment used, the final properties required and the end use of the printed cloth. For example, it is more practical to print on denim sports clothes or on athletic shirts with pigment-type emulsions than it would be to use complex dyes, since generally the end use of these items do not warrant such printing. Inks such as flexible lacquers and oil-vehicle inks may be used directly from the original container for printing and producing signs on satin cloth which are to be used only once for point-of-purchase displays. On the other hand, if the printer is planning to print repeat patterns on bolts of silk, wool or cotton in multicolor designs for an exclusive trade, and the fabric is to withstand the various tests normally given dyed cloth, then precise care and planning must be used on the part of the printer in the printing operation which is part of a more complete and complex process. From a practical angle, the screen-printed patterns should last at least as long as the fabric on which they are printed. This involves pre-printing and post-printing steps.

The treatment given to cloth before printing is governed by the fiber composition of the cloth and depends on the end use of the product. New finishes for fabrics and new fabrics are continually introduced by the textile industry. These fabrics are given treatments at the mills or in the large screen-printing plants, to free them from impurities which may interfere with dye printing. The treatment given may vary from a mild scouring or washing to singeing (boiling off loose hair from the cloth), general boiling or bleaching. The cloth to be printed should be clean whether it is fastened to a hand-printing table or to an endless blanket on a screen-printing textile machine. While ordinarily cloth purchased by the printer should be ready for printing, sometimes it might not be.

In screen-printing on raw silk, difficulties may arise, since raw silk contains a gum known as siricin and therefore the silk must be degummed. This is also one of the reasons that raw silk, when used as a screen fabric, must be thoroughly cleaned before the application of an emulsion or a screen-printing film to it. Likewise, raw wool may contain impurities such as grease, dirt or perspiration. The printer, when purchas-

41

ing textiles, must make sure that the cloth has been treated at the mill, and that it is ready for dye printing. If in doubt, the best procedure is to print a representative sample of the material under the same standardized conditions that the complete job will be done. The sample printing will show existing problems, should there be any, and eliminate final printing difficulties.

Manufacturers in various parts of the world market thousands of dye products for the dye and textile-printing industry. Generally, there is no difference between dye pastes, consisting of the same chemical ingredients, manufactured in one part of the world and those in another. Though these may be the same chemical compounds, they do have different trade names, depending on the manufacturer. Because there seems to be an overabundance of trade names (as in the plastics field), the novice may find the trade nomenclature to be a problem. However, when a certain dye was discovered in 1865 it was sold as "Bismark brown," and not as "benzene-metadiazo-bis-methaphenyl-enediamine dihydrochloride." Synthetic dye products are so complicated chemically that it would be impossible to market all of them under their chemical names. Should the printer have a specific need for the chemical names, they are generally available from the manufacturer.

Classification of Dyes

Dyes are classified according to their color, source, chemical structure and method of application. As far as the source is concerned, dyes may be classified as natural (those obtained from vegetable and mineral sources) or as synthetic (those manufactured or synthesized from raw materials and chemicals). However, the more common method of classifying them is according to their method of application. The processor must realize that the following terms and definitions have been simplified somewhat, because volumes would be required to treat each of the different types of dyes and its properties fully.

Direct printing, mordant printing (mordanting), basic dyes, acid dyes and vat-dye printing are some examples of the varied dye pastes, and the ways that they may be printed on cloth. In direct printing, dye colors are formulated so that they are printed directly, generally on white cloth. The printing paste is compounded so that it does not combine chemically with the cloth until steaming is used to fix the dye onto the cloth. Direct dyes do not require a mordanting process.

In mordant printing, the print paste contains the dye paste and a substance known as a "mordant" (usually a metallic oxide) which facilitates the fixing of the dye and combines with certain dyestuffs to form an insoluble "color lake," or a water-insoluble compound, on the fiber. A mordant dye depends on the presence of a "mordant" for the dyeing action. Mordant dyes are also known as chrome dye pastes. Like other dye pastes, they are available for screen printing and may be prepared. The fabric may be treated with a mordant before, during or after the dyeing process; ordinarily in printing, the mordant is included in the printing paste. When a mordant is printed on a cloth, and the cloth is run through the dye, the mordanted areas will have a different color than the rest of the cloth.

Acid dyes consist of salts of organic acids, and are normally applied to protein fibers, wool, silk and polyamide fibers from an acid bath. Basic dyes consist of salts of organic or color bases.

Vat dyes are synthetic organic dyes available in both paste and powder forms. The term "vat" comes from the fact that originally, in the making of the old indigo dyes, the dyestuff had to steep or ferment in a large vessel or vat before it could be used. Vat dyes are superior dyes. Vat dyes and pastes are not soluble in water alone. Upon application they have no affinity for the cloth. During the steaming operation the vat dye paste changes to a "leuco" form (a water-soluble compound) which is absorbed by the fiber. The printed cloth is then oxidized, and the reaction reverses to form the original water-insoluble color which is left on the fiber.

For using the above dye pastes and other types of dyes such as azoic dyes, sulphur, discharge pastes and pigment-type dyes, the dye manufacturer and the screen-printing supplier offer specific instructions for the preparation, printing, drying, steaming or aging and other steps.

Pigment-Type Inks or Dyes

Pigment-type ink or dye paste originated in the United States* in 1938, and is a common dye-type used for screen-printing on textiles. Pigments used as dyes in screen printing are finely divided, pulverized particles which contribute color and other properties, and are insoluble in the vehicle, carrier or coating material in which the pigments are mixed. They have no affinity for any fiber; the pigment color is fixed onto the fiber by a suitable binder or carrier. The fastness properties of a print made with pigment-type dyes or inks dependent on the type of binder that binds the pigment in a tough film around the individual fibers. Pigment-type colors have answered the problem of printing on textiles which are blends or mixtures of fabrics, because, usually when printing or localized dye is used, these fabrics need mixtures of different types of dyes.

Pigments include white, colored and transparent particles of mineral and synthetic origin, very finely ground and dispersed in a synthetic resin

*The "Aridye" composition with synthetic resin binder was produced by the Inmont Corp.

43

carrier. Transparent pigments, sometimes called extenders, may be used to add bulk to other pigments. The screen- printing manufacturer or supplier will specify what type of binder to use with a particular type of pigment, when it becomes essential for the printer to mix these. The pigment inks are generally of the transparent-type, and the range of shades available is unlimited because the dyes may be mixed with each other. Color pigments are visible from the very beginning, so it is not necessary to heat-cure them before the color is visible.

Pigment-type dyes are classified according to the medium in which the pigment is mixed or dispersed. There are four general types of insoluble pigments which may be printed (mechanically bonded) on textile fibers by means of a carrier or a bonding medium: (1) Water-in-oil emulsion consists of pigments dispersed in a solution of synthetic resin in an organic solvent. The emulsion is produced by the addition of water, at high-speed mixing, to the above ingredients. (2) Oil-in-water emulsion consists of an emulsion which is water and a dispersion of pigments in a solvent solution containing the bonding agent. In the above two types, the printed cloth is dried, then heat-cured in order to bind the bonding medium to the cloth. In the oil-in-water emulsion type, the emulsion may be diluted with the addition of water. (3) Aqueous dispersion consists of pigments dispersed with the aid of a dispersing agent in a solution of a water-soluble binding medium; the medium changes to a water-insoluble form when the printed cloth is steamed or heat-cured. (4) Solvent-soluble or solvent-dispersion pigment-type dye consists of pigments dispersed with the aid of a dispersing agent in a solvent solution containing a solvent-soluble binding agent. These colors do not require steaming or heat-curing.

Pigment-type inks are used for all types of screen-printing on various textiles. They may be used directly from the original container, or they are available in concentrated colors which are mixed in specific proportions with an extender or carrier for the color. Pigment dye inks may also be thinned, be made to produce shades and tints, have additives added to reduce "crocking" or rubbing off of the color through abrasion and may use retarders to slow the drying rate of the printing emulsion. However, to obtain the best results, the fabric should be free of interfering sizes and finishing agents. Also, the printer should follow directions in storing the pigment inks which have been formulated and mixed by him, from ingredients supplied by a dyestuff manufacturer. As with other types of dye printing, it is suggested that the printer make a complete trial printing, if he has any doubts about the quality of a specific pigment dye or ink.

The development of binders that set with the aid of heat spurred great growth in the textile screen-printing industry. While there are other binders, water-soluble aminoaldehydes and solvent-soluble ureas, and melamine formaldehyde resins are most often used. The main advan-

44

tage of the pigment dyes is that they require only two operations after printing—drying or driving off the volatile materials, and heat-curing or fixing the binder in order to set the color. There are other advantages: the purchased dye ink may be used directly from the container, or the color may be easily mixed by the printer. The colors have excellent fastness to light, to washing and to dry cleaning. They may be combined with one another in any proportion to produce a variety of shades and tints, although it is suggested that only colors of the same manufacturer be mixed. They may be printed on the same cloth with other types of dyes. Their post-treatment is limited usually to heat-curing and they are easy to clean off the printing screen. Also, they print detail and can be printed on practically any natural, synthetic or blend fiber. Pigment-type dye screen-printing inks, of course, may also be printed on materials other than textiles.

Preparation for Printing

The preparation of these pigment dyes for either hand or machine printing is simple. High-speed mixers are necessary when the printer wants to prepare the carrier or binder, and then add the concentrated colors to produce the paste for printing. Manufacturers supply formulations for mixing in proportions of parts of gallons, hundredths or thousandths.

Dyes for printing are formulated with thickening agents to obtain satisfactory viscosity and sharpness of printing, and to prevent blurring effects. By using the correct thickener, screen printing can produce a deposit heavy enough to print on floor rugs. In addition to preventing the spreading of the printed pattern, the thickener acts as a medium for easy transfer of the dye to the cloth. The composition of the print paste is an important factor in screen printing. Manufacturers supply thickeners for mixing and formulating print pastes and also ingredients for the processor to mix the thickener. Like dyes, mixed thickeners have taken years to evolve. It is suggested that the novice experiment, and mix as little as possible of the thickener at first.

Because thickeners affect cloth penetration, the wrong gum or ingredient may interfere with the fixing of the dyestuff onto the cloth, may not wash out easily or may cause mark-off or offset. The printer must realize that particular types of thickeners or mixtures are used with particular types of colors. There are thickening agents which are used and removed from the printed cloth without affecting the colors. There are also compounds which serve as thickeners because different thickeners produce different effects in printing.

The following are used in screen printing as gums and thickening agents, and may be employed alone or in combination, depending on what is required: sodium alginate, textile gum, locust bean gum, gum tragacanth, carboxymethyl cellulose, hydroethyl cellulose, British gum, dextrine and modified gums and starches. There is no one thickener that can be used for all purposes. Much more thickener is applied in screen printing than is used in machine roller printing. However, dye and chemical concentrations are usually decreased for screen printing. Often the thickener may consist of needed ingredients for printing to which specific proportions of color are added. For example, the following printing-paste formulation* of vat colors for printing on nylon calls for

15 parts dye
85 parts thickener
_____
100 parts total

However, the thickener in the above formulation consists of the following ingredients:

a. 100 parts potassium carbonate
b. 100 parts Sulfoxite C
c. 50 parts glycerin
d. 100 parts water
e. 650 parts textile gum or British gum (50%)
_____
1000 parts total

Figure 28. **An ink, paint and dye-paste mixer of five-gallon (18.93 liter) capacity which rotates on a turntable. (Courtesy of Naz-Dar Company, Chicago IL)**

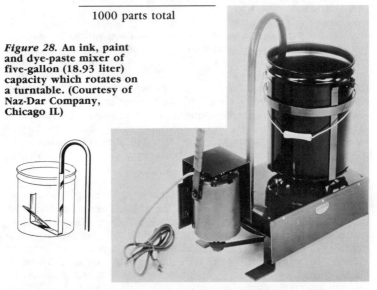

Dyes and Chemicals Division, E.I. Du Pont de Nemours and Co., Inc., Wilmington, Del. Other formulations for specific dye products are available from the following manufacturers: 1. Celanese Fibers Co., Charlotte, NC; 2. Ciba-Geigy Corp., Greensboro, NC; 3. ICI United States, Inc., Charlotte, NC; 4. Colors and Chemicals Division, Inmont Corp., Hawthorne, NJ; 5. General Aniline and Film Corp., New York, NY; 6. Polymer Industries, Inc., Springdale, Conn.

46

Generally, the ingredients are added in the order given and are mixed with a high-speed mixer. Figure 28 presents a mixer used by printers for general mixing, and which may be used for experimental mixing. After the above printing-paste formulation is mixed, and the cloth printed, the prints are dried, then aged or steamed for five to ten minutes in a rapid ager unit, oxidized for three to five minutes in a bath containing twenty percent sodium perborate or hydrogen peroxide, acidified with 0.5 percent acetic acid at 140 to 160 degrees Fahrenheit (60 to 71 degrees Celsius) and soaped at 140 degrees Fahrenheit (60 degrees Celsius). The above is not presented to stress the complexity of dye printing, since screen printing is generally not this complex, but to show that formulations often include post-treating specifications.

While it is not suggested that the beginner prepare thickeners, Figure 29 presents formulations for the preparations of some thickeners should the processor have need for them. Gum arabic (gum Senegal), gum tragacanth, locust bean gum and wheat starch are used as the ingredients. Gums are of vegetable or plant origin and are available in flake and powder form. They are generally prepared first by soaking (usually 1000 parts) and straining. Boiling is done in a double-boiler or in a steam or water-jacketed boiler. These swell when heated in water and a viscous or adhesive mixture is produced. With some gums (locust bean) a germicide is added to prevent mold or bacterial growth in storage. This type of thickener should be used right after it is mixed. The proportion of the dye mixed and stirred in these thickeners would depend on the recommendation of the dye manufacturer, on experimentation and on standardized procedures developed by the printer as a result of objective testing.

It is encouraging that the manufacturers and suppliers in various parts of the world have developed formulations that may be mixed by the printer under normal but controlled shop conditions.

PREPARATION OF SOME THICKENERS*

Thickener	Preparation for Use
A. Gum Tragacanth	(1) Mix 70 parts of gum tragacanth in 1000 parts of cold water. (2) Allow mixture to stand for 2 to 3 days with occasional stirring. (3) Then boil mixture until gum is dissolved; this may take from 4 to 12 hours. (4) Cool, bulk or measure to 1000 parts (by volume), and strain. This preparation is a 7% mixture.
B. Wheat Starch and Gum Tragacanth	(1) Stir 140 parts of wheat starch into 400 parts of cold water. (2) Add 600 parts of gum tragacanth (7% mixture as explained above) and stir. (3) Boil whole mixture for 30 to 40 minutes, stirring constantly. (4) Cool, bulk to 1000 parts and strain.
C. Gum Arabic (Gum Senegal)	(1) Stir 600 parts of this gum into 500 parts of water. (2) Measure off mixture to 1000 parts and boil with constant stirring for about 3 hours. (3) Cool, bulk to 1000 parts and strain.
D. Locust Bean Gum (St. John's Bread)	(1) Dissolve 0.5 parts of borax in 1000 parts of water. (2) Then add 20 parts of gum with constant stirring. (3) Add a little acetic acid to make thickening slightly acid and heat mixture at 175-195 degrees Fahrenheit. (4) Add a trace of phenol to prevent mould growth. (5) Cool thickener, bulk to 1000 parts and strain.

*Mixture proportions courtesy of Imperial Chemical Industries Ltd., Manchester, England.

Figure 29. **Some thickeners and their preparation for use.**

Chapter VI

TREATMENT OF TEXTILES AFTER SCREEN PRINTING

This writer has an abiding faith in the future of screen printing as a process, because it contributes to so many related graphic arts methods. At the same time, screen printing is forced to adopt the methods of related industries when the process is used to decorate materials. Thus, the post-treatment of screen-printed textile cloth is similar to the post-treatment of textile materials printed by other processes.

The printer who specializes in textile screen printing will be performing drying and heat-curing or fixation of the print as post-treatment of the printed cloth. He may also be involved with other post-treatment processes such as steaming, aging, soaping, washing and finishing, as specified in the formulation he will be using for textile printing.

Drying the printed cloth is very important, because drying the wet paste prevents mark-off or the offset of the wet printed design onto the unprinted portions. While in general, drying will not fix the printed pattern onto the cloth, there are some screen-printing pigment inks which will become fixed if allowed to air-dry for a period of three to four weeks. This, however, is not practical for the average shop. Hand screen-printed items may be hung dry; machine-printed cloth is usually machine-dried. In machine screen printing, the drying is synchronized with the printing by means of a drying unit that is attached to the machine. The cloth may also be dried by being festooned or suspended in loops as illustrated in Figure 30. The rods for festooning may be fastened or hung from the ceiling so that they do not occupy floor space, or they may be built on a portable unit, allowing the festooner to be moved away into an airy area or in front of fans. The cloth should be hung as illustrated, so that the prints do not mark-off onto the unprinted portions. The festoon principle is also employed in festoon steamers. These suspend the cloth in loops and move it through the air-free steaming conditions through the machine.

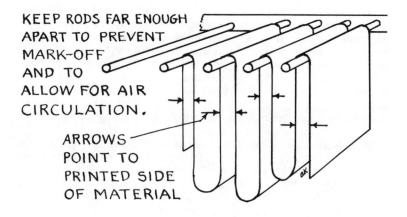

KEEP RODS FAR ENOUGH
APART TO PREVENT
MARK-OFF
AND TO
ALLOW FOR AIR
CIRCULATION.

ARROWS
POINT TO
PRINTED SIDE
OF MATERIAL

Figure 30. **Festooning printed cloth for drying.**

A hot room with circulating air may also be employed for drying screen-printed pieces; heated tables may be used for hand printing. Textile-printing shops which do a lot of printing may use heated drying revolving cylinders, arranged vertically or horizontally, for drying the printed material as it passes around the cylinders. They may be internally heated with steam, and the number of cylinders used depends on the material to be dried. Various heat-applying units may be used in screen-printing shops, as illustrated in Figures 31 and 32, the most common units being the convection-type ovens and infrared machines. Either of these may be built to the specifications of individual shops, allowing for differing speeds and temperatures.

Infrared drying machines are generally designed so that the lamps operate only when the conveyor is in motion, since printed cloth may burn if kept under the lamps too long a time. While these are called drying machines, they are also used for heat-curing or setting some printed colors. Screen-printed pigment-type dyes usually require three to seven minutes for heat-curing prints at 250 to 350 degrees Fahrenheit (121 to 177 degrees Celsius) depending on the type of ink. The higher the temperature, the less is the time needed for curing. It is suggested that the printer heat-cure a sample of yardage first, especially of those fabrics that contain synthetic fibers, and check it for tendering effects (deterioration of textile fiber), before heat-curing it on a commercial scale, since dark colors tend to absorb infrared rays very rapidly and the printed cloth may be damaged. Screen prints must be dried well before being steamed or aged.

49

As has been mentioned, screen-printing pigment colors do not have to be steamed. They may be air-dried from 30 minutes to one hour, depending on the absorbency and thickness of the ink deposit. Or the printed material may be force-dried for about two minutes at 140 to 200 degrees Fahrenheit (60 to 93 degrees Celsius). However, to obtain the best properties, the printed textile material should be heat-cured at any of the following temperatures and time lengths: 275 degrees Fahrenheit (135 degrees Celsius) for five minutes; 300 degrees Fahrenheit (149 degrees Celsius) for three minutes; or 375 degrees Fahrenheit (190 degrees Celsius) for two minutes. Any type of dryer that is used for drying textile-printed material may be employed. (See Figures 31 and 32)

While convection dryers have been used and still are used, recently the screen printer began to employ a flash-cure or spot-cure unit for items such as jackets and garments (See Figures 63A, 68, 68A and 69). These pedestal units, under which the garment passes, are practical for the quick application of heat to freshly printed garments, and quickly create a surface for the application of the next color.

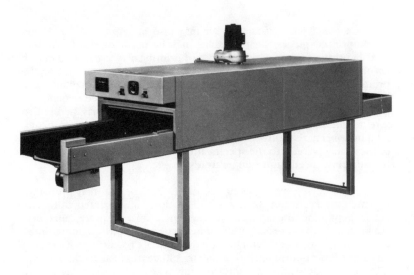

Figure 31. An Eir-Econ Infrared Textile Dryer designed for drying and curing textile inks, plastisols, heat transfers, epoxies, enamels and other polymerizing materials. The unit is of modular construction allowing for the addition of extra heat modules, and has a variable-speed conveyor with a width of 34″ to 48″ (86cm to 122cm). (Courtesy of Cincinnati Screen Process Supplies, Inc., Cincinnati, OH)

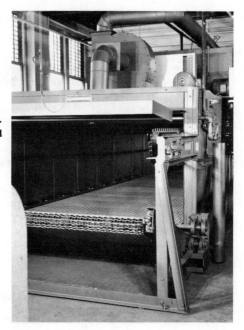

Figure 32. A two-zone, gas-fired Grieve-Hendry oven with work space dimensions six feet (1.83m) wide, 45 feet (14.72m) long, and four feet (1.22m) high. The oven is designed for drying and heat-curing screen-printed items on a roller chain rod conveyor at the top of the oven and a mesh belt conveyor at the bottom. Speed and temperature up to 600 degrees Fahrenheit (316 Celsius) may be controlled. (Courtesy of Excello, Ltd., Chicago, IL)

After the cloth is dry, the dye-printed pattern must be fixed to the cloth by steaming, or some other method of heat application. If steaming, heat-curing or aging specifications are not furnished by the dye manufacturer, the processor must arrive at them by a trial-and-error method. The heat, especially the temperature of the steam, causes the ingredients in the print to form insoluble compounds on the fibers of the cloth, so that the print becomes more or less permanent.

Different dyes require different temperatures and times. During steaming, the printed areas absorb moisture and (as in dyeing) form a concentrated dye bath spot in the printed area. The thickening agent in the print prevents the dyestuff from spreading during the steaming operation. Dyes such as acid, basic, mordant, discharge, direct and vat are each affected differently by steam. Therefore, the steaming operation must be controlled; the steam must not be too moist or too dry. The temperature of the steaming or heating period will vary with the type of dye printed.

In aging (ageing) or steaming, the printed fabric is given a treatment of moist steam in the absence of air, or the fabric may be exposed to a hot moist atmosphere, not necessarily air-free. The purpose of the application of heat, steaming or aging the print, is to fix the colors upon the fibers, to assist the various ingredients in the formulation to react

51

correctly and to remove the "hand" (hardness or stiffness) from the print. The fixation or development of the dye in prints may be done under pressure in cottage steamers, by steaming at atmospheric pressure, may be done in an ager or steam chamber or by using dry heat. The type of fabric being printed, the dye or ink printed and the type of equipment used determine the post-treatment of the printed cloth. Some sources of equipment for the fixation and steaming of prints are screen-printing manufacturers and suppliers, manufacturers of automatic screen-printing textile equipment and manufacturers of general textile-printing and dyeing equipment. With pigment-type inks, the stiffness of the print will generally disappear after the product is washed by the comsumer. The application of heat aids in the production of colors of more impact, colors which are fast and restitant to various tests, aids in discharging or removing a printed pattern from a uniformly dyed background, and in general produces prints of a more permanent nature so that the print will last at least as long as the item printed.

The beginner may find that hanging the textile items for twelve to 24 hours in a warm, humid atmosphere may aid in fixing the dried print to the cloth. For some sample prints, the processor may fix the prints by hand-ironing for three to five minutes over both sides of the design, using a damp cloth under the medium-hot iron. A domestic or kitchen oven can also be used for fixing the dye print.

For experimental and small-volume heat application, the processor may use the same heat-curing method as that employed by the batik printer. In this method, several lengths of a fabric may be steamed at the same time by separating each length with several sheets of newsprint paper, so that one layer of cloth does not touch the other. Clean cotton or back grey cloth may be used instead of newsprint paper. The paper should be laid on a table or the floor, and the printed cloth placed on the paper so that the paper overlaps all sides of the cloth. The ends of the paper sticking out should be folded and tied. The whole may be covered with a back grey cloth or a blanket and hung or placed in a steamer of the type illustrated in Figure 33, and steamed for a minimum of one hour. It is suggested that the roll of fabric and paper not be made too tight, in order to allow the heat to better penetrate. With these types of steaming arrangements, steaming may be done for a slightly longer time than that recommended. After the cloth is removed, washed in warm water and rinsed until the thickening paste is removed, it may be stretched, dried and ironed or mangled.

Shops specializing in textile screen printing use several types of agers for steaming and aging. The beginner may use a steaming unit of the type suggested in Figure 33 which can be made of a metal garbage or dust bin, a metal drum or even from a large galvanized metal pail. This unit, depending on the size the printer plans to build or have built, can be used for experimental steaming and even for some commercial steam-

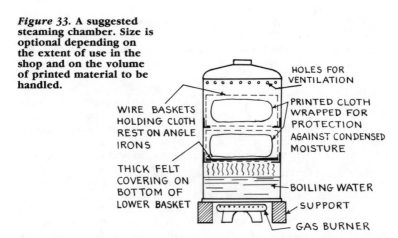

Figure 33. **A suggested steaming chamber. Size is optional depending on the extent of use in the shop and on the volume of printed material to be handled.**

HOLES FOR VENTILATION

WIRE BASKETS HOLDING CLOTH REST ON ANGLE IRONS

PRINTED CLOTH WRAPPED FOR PROTECTION AGAINST CONDENSED MOISTURE

THICK FELT COVERING ON BOTTOM OF LOWER BASKET

BOILING WATER

SUPPORT

GAS BURNER

ing. The water being heated should be filled to about one-fifth or one-fourth the height of the steamer; the water should not boil out before the steaming period is finished. The unit may be built with a faucet for drawing off water at the bottom of the bin, and with an overflow pipe at the side, allowing the water to remain at a certain height in the container. The thick felt, shown in the illustration, at the bottom of the lower basket may be removed should it become desirable to allow the steam to ascend more freely. The ventilation holes are necessary, allowing the escape of a certain amount of steam and the decomposed products that may form during the steaming process.

In these homemade units, the printer must make sure that a flow of steam is maintained at all times, and that condensation is controlled to prevent the condensed steam particles from forming into water and penetrating through the cloth being steamed. If water should condense on the inside of the bin cover, several thicknesses of felt may be placed over the can, with the cover placed on top of the felt. The felt will absorb the condensed steam, preventing a downpour over the printed cloth. The fabric may be steamed once to heat-cure several printed colors at the same time, but the colors must be dry before being steamed.

Ultimately, the printer who specializes in textile screen printing will have to purchase a steamer or have one built to fit his needs. Probably, this will be a cottage steamer, rapid ager or tower or vertical ager. Although the name "cottage" is derived from the earlier steamers which were shaped like a cottage, the modern cottage steamer is generally cylindrically-shaped with a door at one end of the cylinder for loading the dyed or printed matter. In the type of steamer known as the continuous steaming chamber or ager, the cloth is festooned on rods and may be steamed up to 60 minutes, depending on conditions. In the rapid ager, the cloth travels over the horizontal rollers at the top and bottom,

53

and travels through the steam area in three to ten minutes, depending on the cloth and the dye formula used. The rapid ager consists of a rectangular housing with horizontal rollers at the top and bottom of the housing or chamber. Most rapid agers require volume production to be economical.

The vertical, tower or chimney ager illustrated in Figure 34 is often used by screen printers, and is one of the most important pieces of equipment in printing with vat and other dyes which require heat-curing. Instead of being vertical, the ager may take the form of a straight horizontal shape or be shaped like the inverted "U" illustrated in Figure 35. This ager prevents mark-off which is important in screen printing, because of the thick amounts of color deposited. Also, the face of the print does not come into contact with the rollers or bars inside the ager. While the height of the vertical ager depends on the length of the cloth used, usually the tower is 30 to 40 feet in height. This type of ager is equipped with entrance and exit slots and freely-running rollers at the top. The ager is designed to maintain an atmosphere of steam. The steam is introduced at the bottom of the ager through perforated coils into water boxes. The cloth enters at the bottom (see Figure 34), passes to the top over a roller, returns to the bottom and leaves the ager without the printed side ever touching any object or roller inside the unit.

Figure 35 presents a flash ager. Flash-aging produces very rapid dye fixation on screen-printed fabrics, especially with vat dyes.

The processes of printing and aging described here are becoming routine procedures in screen-printing shops doing automatic screen printing.

***Figure 34.* A vertical tower ager designed for aging screen-printed vat colors and steaming other types of dye colors. (Courtesy of Ciba-Geigy Corp., Greensboro, NC)**

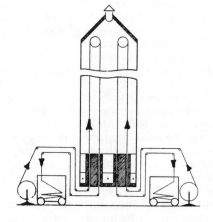

Figure 35. A flash ager of inverted "U" construction used for aging screen-printed goods in twenty seconds, at about 30 yards (27.43m) per minute and at 225 to 230 degrees Fahrenheit (107 to 110 Celsius). The printed goods pass into a vertical slot, then go through a horizontal heating chamber, pass through the exit slot and into the water and other finishing processes, before moving to the dryer. (Courtesy of Tower Iron Works, Inc., Seekong, MA)

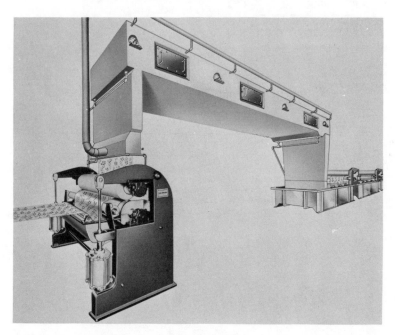

The final treatment after steaming or aging depends on the type of dye being printed. Generally, after steaming, the cloth may require warm or cold water rinsing to remove thickening, surplus unfixed dyes and chemicals. Some printed cloth is given a soaping treatment and rinsed and dried in addition to other finishing treatments, again depending on the recommendation of the dye manufacturer, and on the type of cloth being printed. As an example of post-treatment, Figure 36 presents a flow chart which shows an arrangement of machines or processing units for treating vat-type dye screen-printed cloth. With this type of dye paste, the cloth, after being printed, passes quickly and uniformly through a padder (a mangle or special set of rollers) which has a trough containing a special solution of chemicals which impregnate the cloth, completing the printing process. The dye, after passing through the padder, is fixed as quickly as possible by aging or heat-curing in a pressure chest or ager of the type shown in Figure 37. Upon leaving the ager, the cloth passes through an open-width washer where cold water rinses off as much of the chemicals as possible. After being washed, the cloth passes through an oxidizing bath, followed by a rinsing bath, is soaped vigorously, washed again and finally goes to a dryer.

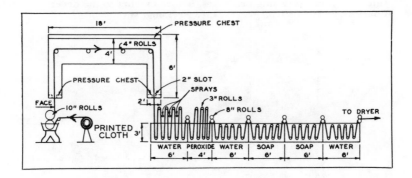

Figure 36. An arrangement of machines for padding, aging, finishing and drying cloth that has been screen-printed with vat-type dyes. (Courtesy of Textile Industries Magazine, Atlanta, GA)

Chapter VII

GENERAL DESCRIPTION OF PRINTING SCREENS FOR TEXTILE PRINTING

As an evolving industry matures, the focus of its growth is on improving and refining its processes to answer immediate industrial needs. Therefore, it is necessary to understand the standardized and accepted techniques and principles before becoming involved industrially with more complex processing. Various types of screen-printing plates or printing screens have been used for printing designs on textiles since the 1930s. However, the printing screens used today to apply multicolored patterns and to decorate fabrics include different types of photographic screens, hand-prepared knife-cut film screens and tusche-glue or resist-type screens. While all three types can be used commercially, the photographic and the knife-cut film screens are used more often. Tusche-glue screens are used more for hand printing, for teaching purposes, for avocational pursuits and for non-volume work. All of these screens may be used for printing on any surface, although for some textile printing, the screens may need reinforcing with certain agents or compounds to increase their resistance to the solvent effects of the chemicals in the dye pastes. All three types may be used for manual, semi-automatic and machine printing.

The preparation of a printing screen consists of leaving the design area open in the fabric mesh, which should be stretched taut on a frame, and filling-in the rest of the screen fabric with a resist, filler or block-out solution which will resist, and not be dissolved by, the dye paste being printed in the screen. The materials used for the preparation of textile-printing screens have been standardized, and are available in various parts of the world from screen-printing suppliers and manufacturers, from graphic arts supply houses and from art supply firms.

Even though photographic printing screens produce any desired effect and are therefore the most frequently used, hand-prepared screens are still sometimes employed in textile screen printing. Because the beginning printer may find the preparation of hand-prepared screens simpler, a description of the two hand-prepared screens—knife-cut and tusche or resist—is presented first*.

Knife-cut Film Screens

Knife-cut film consists of a transparent or translucent film semipermanently attached to a thin transparent or translucent backing sheet made of thin plastic or paper. (The paper backing sheet film is being used less and less for textile printing.) The film on the backing sheet is available in various transparent colors and thicknesses to facilitate printing the

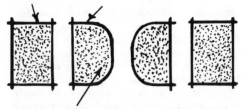

KNIFE CUTS EXTEND
PAST CORNERS

DESIGN PARTS OF FILM
ARE PEELED OFF

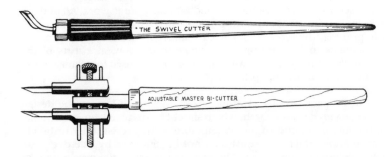

Figure 38. **A swivel cutter for making single-line cuts, and an adjustable bi-cutter for cutting two parallel lines at one time. (Courtesy of Naz-Dar Company, Chicago, IL)**

---

*Hand-prepared printing screens are treated more completely in the book: Kosloff, Albert, *Screen Printing Techniques.* Signs of the Times Publishing Company, Cincinnati, Ohio.

different thicknesses of dye inks on textiles. Film is available in many size sheets and rolls of different widths and lengths, allowing the printer to prepare any size printing screen. When cut and adhered correctly, knife-cut films produce a screen that will print thousands of impressions. The development of knife-cut film in 1930 and 1931 did more for the growth of screen printing than any other product at that time. It offered a printing screen that could be prepared by the processor, that could print on any surface, could be removed from the screen fabric and could print sharp lines with a variety of inks.

Generally, the films are adhered to the underside of the screen fabric with a solvent that varies with the type of film used. For example, lacquer-type films are adhered with a lacquer solvent usually available from the supplier of the film, while water-soluble films are adhered with water or water and isopropyl alcohol. Lacquer-type films are used to print oil-vehicle-type dye inks, water-soluble dyes and pastes and dye inks with some water in them. Water-soluble hand-cut film is employed for printing almost any type of ink paste except those containing water. Basically, the film or filler used for the printing screen must resist, and not be dissolved by, the ink printed.

The film is prepared for printing by taping or fastening it over the design, film side up, and cutting and peeling it away from the design areas, leaving the rest of the film intact. In cutting with the film or stencil knife, the cuts must continue a little past the corners, as shown in Figure 37, or the film will not peel off correctly. The cutting must be done with razor-sharp knives or cutting instruments (see Figures 38, 39 and 40), and one must be careful to cut only through the film and not the backing sheet. Cutting the backing sheet will make it more difficult to adhere the film to the screen fabric.

After the design is cut and the film peeled away in the design areas, the film with the backing sheet is attached, in perfect contact, under the screen with a solvent recommended by the manufacturer of the film. The best method of doing this is to place the film on a build-up layer of the type shown in Figure 41—a flat cardboard or other panel or glass about 1/8 inch to 3/8 inch thick. The screen is then placed and held on top of the layer, ensuring complete contact over the entire surface of the film. All areas of the film must be in contact with the screen fabric. To adhere, a small area of the fabric is wetted on the inside over the film with an adhering liquid, and wiped off immediately with a clean soft dry cloth. When working on a large film, small portions at a time should be wetted and dried, wiping off immediately after each liquid application. The printer should start at one side of the screen and work in the same direction to avoid wrinkles. This adhering procedure is a standard today, in the application of film to fabric with solvents. The adhering liquid should soften the film just enough for the fabric to adhere permanently to the film without dissolving the sharp knife-cut edges on

59

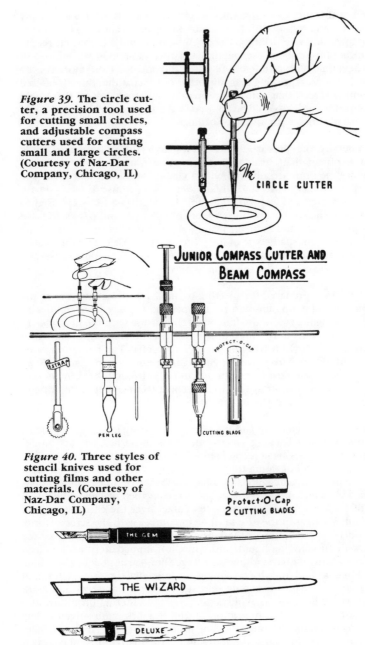

Figure 39. The circle cutter, a precision tool used for cutting small circles, and adjustable compass cutters used for cutting small and large circles. (Courtesy of Naz-Dar Company, Chicago, IL)

CIRCLE CUTTER

JUNIOR COMPASS CUTTER AND BEAM COMPASS

PROTECT-O-CAP

EXTRA

PEN LEG

CUTTING BLADE

Figure 40. Three styles of stencil knives used for cutting films and other materials. (Courtesy of Naz-Dar Company, Chicago, IL)

Protect-O-Cap
2 CUTTING BLADES

THE GEM

THE WIZARD

DELUXE

it.

The film should dry thoroughly (it dries in about ten minutes depending on atmospheric conditions); a fan may be used to hasten the drying process. When the film has dried and adhered well to the screen fabric, the backing sheet can be peeled away, with the film bearing the design left on the bottom of the screen. The rest of the screen fabric is filled-in with a filler or blockout solution, and the screen is ready for printing. If a part of the backing sheet does not peel off easily because it hasn't completely dried, wet the screen over that part, holding it flat and giving it enough time to dry before continuing to peel.

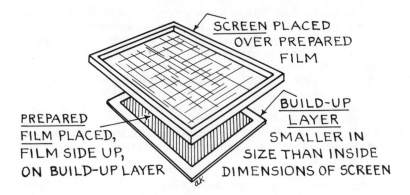

SCREEN PLACED OVER PREPARED FILM

PREPARED FILM PLACED, FILM SIDE UP, ON BUILD-UP LAYER

BUILD-UP LAYER SMALLER IN SIZE THAN INSIDE DIMENSIONS OF SCREEN

Figure 41. Using a build-up layer to obtain better contact when adhering film to the screen fabric.

On occasion shellacked or lacquered papers are used for textile printing. These papers are cut in the same fashion as film, except that the cutting is done through the coating and the paper. Knife-cut papers are adhered with a solvent; shellacked paper can be adhered with a solvent or ironed onto the screen with a medium-hot iron. Before cutting, the design may be drawn or traced onto the paper.

The commercial-type knife-cut films are very tough, produce sharp prints, are not difficult to prepare, produce fine detail depending on the skill of the film cutter and will last for thousands of impressions if prepared and applied correctly. After use, the film can be removed from the screen with cleaning solvents available from any screen-printing supply firm. As with any other screen-preparation medium, the ink must be cleaned off the screen completely before removing the film.

One of the most practical ways to remove knife-cut film is to place several sheets of newspaper between the screen and the base (or table).

Then, holding the screen in a flat position, saturate the inside of the screen with a cloth dipped in the correct solvent. After several minutes, lift up the screen very quickly. The film will adhere to the newspaper. If necessary, repeat the procedure.

Because some of the solvents used for cleaning off ink and removing films are flammable, it is suggested that care be exercised in their use. Shops which clean many screens daily usually have screen washing machines or units. These devices filter and use the same solvents over and over, reducing clean-up time.

Tusche-Glue or Washout Screen

In the tusche-glue, resist or washout screen, another hand-prepared screen that was one of the first used for textile screen printing, two fillers are employed in the preparation—a temporary filler, resist or masking medium and a more permanent or background filler. The temporary filler, usually a substance known as "tusche," is a special greasy, black substance available as a liquid or solid that may be applied in liquid, stick or crayon form to the screen fabric. The textile design to be reproduced is placed under the screen and traced onto the screen fabric with a pencil or pen. The tusche is applied carefully and thoroughly only over the design areas of the fabric. When the tusche is dry, the other, more permanent filler is applied over the tusche and the rest of the screen fabric (see Figure 42).

Glue is the permanent filler usually used, because it is easily available and may be washed off with water when it is necessary to reclaim the screen. Also, it resists all inks except water-soluble types. The glue used generally is a liquid glue that is mixed with water—one part glue to one part water. The consistency of the glue or background filler should be such that when poured on the screen fabric it will not run through the mesh. Today, in addition to glue, there are other commercial water-soluble screen-blockout mediums which are very practical and which are easy to remove from the screen when necessary. Alkyd screen-process enamels, lacquers, varnishes and special fillers, depending on the type of dye to be printed, are also used as permanent fillers. For example, when printing water-soluble dye inks and some acid-type dye pastes, liquid tusche may be employed for filling in the design and an alkyd screen-process enamel (generally white) may be used for the more permanent filler.

The tusche can be applied with a pen or brush, by spraying on with a spray gun or by drawing the pattern on the screen fabric with a crayon-type tusche. Crayon and pencil-type tusche is available in varying degrees of hardness and softness. The printer must make sure that the tusche covers the design completely. If necessary, after the first coat dries, a second coat may be applied. Liquid tusche is practical for covering the

62

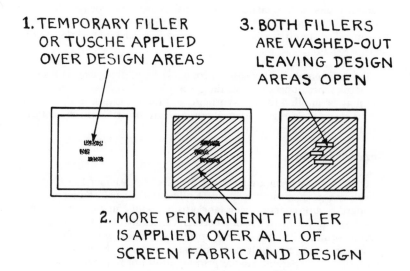

1. TEMPORARY FILLER OR TUSCHE APPLIED OVER DESIGN AREAS

3. BOTH FILLERS ARE WASHED-OUT LEAVING DESIGN AREAS OPEN

2. MORE PERMANENT FILLER IS APPLIED OVER ALL OF SCREEN FABRIC AND DESIGN

Figure 42. **The application of two fillers to prepare a resist or tusche-glue screen.**

solid areas of the design; crayons and tusche pencils may be used to produce shading effects.

When the tusche and the background filler are completely dry, the tusche can be washed off with a solvent such as turpentine, mineral spirits, kerosene or benzine or with a commercial solvent. Tusche is soluble in water before drying; after drying it can be removed with the listed solvents. To dissolve the tusche but not the glue, a cloth soaked in one of the solvents can be rubbed over the tusche areas on the underside of the screen fabric. After the tusche begins to dissolve, the inside of the screen may be rubbed. As the tusche is dissolved and rubbed off with a soft cloth wetted in the same solvent, it will take along the permanent filler covering it, leaving the design areas open for printing.

Some printers cover the underside of the fabric with a thin coating of starch or laundry paste and allow it to dry. Then the tusche is applied on the inside of the screen. The starch or paste coating prevents the tusche from seeping through. This is a good technique to use in the preparation of textile-printing screens, because these screens generally have coarse fabrics. The printer should experiment with the various laundry starches, pastes and adhesives available, to make sure that the dried paste coating can be easily dissolved or wiped off with a wet cloth, and that it does not interfere with the dissolving of the tusche. When permanent fillers such as enamels or varnishes are used, the starch can be easily washed off with water before starting to wash-out the tusche coating. The starch coating may be sprayed on, or squeegeed just once onto the fabric.

Tusche is employed because it produces screens that print with a variety of ink types. It produces shading, spraying, tracing and other effects, and may be applied to silk, synthetic and metal fabrics. It also allows the artist and the designer to create original art directly onto silk without tracing from prepared artwork or copy.

Screen Fabrics

Glue-tusche screens are generally prepared on Number 12 to Number 18 silk or equivalent screen fabrics. Knife-cut film can be adhered to any standard fine or coarse screen fabric from about Number 2 to Number 25 silk or equivalent. While other screen fabrics are employed for general screen printing, textile screen printers usually use multifilament polyester, nylon, monofilament polyester, metal cloth (mostly stainless steel) or silk. Generally, textile printing does not require a fabric finer than mesh that is equivalent to Number 16 silk. It is practical to use the best quality of fabric, and regardless of the type of emulsion coating or film one is applying to it, the fabric must be completely clean before adhering the film or applying the emulsion.

Usage has been, and is, standardizing fabrics into a "number" classification, although there are slight differences in the fabrics manufactured for the trade. Because silk was the first practical fabric used commercially, the other screen cloths are compared with silk. Silk ranges in this classification from Number 0000 to Number 25, with Number 0000 being the coarsest and having about 15 1/2 threads per linear inch, and Number 25 being the finest, having about 195 threads per linear inch and the smallest openings between the threads. To designate the quality of the silk, the number has the letter "X," "XX" or "XXX" after it: ie. 12X, 12XX, or 12XXX. The double-X (XX) quality cloth is usually used for textile printing. By observing Figure 43, the reader will note that the column "No." for silk and multifilament polyester does not indicate the mesh or threads per inch or centimeter. These and other data are normally indicated for the printer on charts.

Although silk may still be used for some textile printing, the multifilaments 6XX through 12XX polyester, and monofilaments 110 through 225 polyester and nylon are more often used. The classification number for nylon, metal cloth or monofilament polyester indicates directly the mesh number or number of threads per linear inch and/or centimeter. Monofilament fabrics are made of one-filament threads, while multifilament fabrics are made of more than one-filament threads. Because of its printing quality, thicker coating deposit, and greater print-

Figure 43. The classification numbers of screen fabrics, mesh count or number of threads per linear inch and percentage of open-area for silk, nylon, stainless steel and multifilament and monofilament polyester.

SILK No.	MESH COUNT	% OPEN AREA	NYLON No.	% OPEN AREA	STAINLESS STEEL No.	% OPEN AREA	POLYESTER (MULTIFILAMENT) No	MESH COUNT	% OPEN AREA	POLYESTER (MONOFILAMENT) No.	% OPEN AREA
2XX	54	54	50	46.5						45	47
4XX	65	49	63	43						63	48
6XX	73	47					6XX	74	47	76	34
7XX	81		83	41	80X80	50	7XX	76	46	83	41
8XX	85	45					8XX	79	45	92	42
9XX	95		90	41.5	100X100	47				103	39
10XX	106	41					10XX	110	40	110	39
11XX	114		114	47.5			11XX	118	36	115	39
12XX	122	33	120	44.5	120X120	47	12XX	125	32	123	39
13XX	127		132	40.5			13XX	135		131	32
14XX	136	31	138	46.5	135X135	47	14XX	138	30	137	35
15XX	144		152	38	145X145	46				148	38
16XX	152	30	149	43			16XX	148	29	156	30
17XX	160		166	38	165X165	47				163	37
18XX	171	29					18XX	168	35		
19XX	175										
20XX	183	28	185	42.5	180X180	47	20XX	175	27	175	34
25XX	195	22	196	44	200X200	46				186	34
			254	32	250X250	36					
			285	37							
∞			306	33	325X325	31					

ing resistance, textile printers have begun to use multifilament polyester more than in the past.

Nylon is available in a range of mesh—from about Number 16 to Number 465; stainless steel comes from 30 to about 500 mesh per inch (30 x 30 openings to 500 x 500 openings per square inch). Phosphor bronze metal cloth and other fabrics are available in practical mesh for the textile printer. Fabrics can be purchased in widths of up to 120 inches (305 cm) and in rolls up to about 60 yards long (54.86m). Thus, the textile printer has his choice of any fabric for printing, in addition to any dye paste or ink and varied thicknesses of ink coatings. He may even use a metalized monofilament polyester fabric which has a resistant metal coating embedded in it.

It is interesting to note, as shown in Figure 43, that unlike silk and multifilament polyester, nylon, stainless steel and monofilament polyester have greater open areas which allow for greater dye-paste deposit during printing. For example, the ink flow through most grades of Number 196 is equal to or greater than that of Number 10XX silk which has 106 threads to the inch. It is obvious that film will adhere better to 196 threads than it will to 106 threads. So finer-detail printing will be obtained with the nylon, all else being equal. However, it must be noted that nylon and stainless steel require more care in their preparation for receiving screen-printing films and coatings. Films and coatings do adhere better to silk.

Although silk standards serve as a guide for comparison, synthetic fabrics such as nylon and polyester do employ a more complete system of measurement. The specifications include: (1) the mesh openings in microns*, or parts of an inch; (2) the open printing area, which is a percentage indicating the total screen surface open for the ink; and (3) the thickness of the fabric, which may vary depending on the mesh count and the thread diameter. Manufacturers suggest that the mesh openings should be at least three times the average pigment grain size.

It must be noted that nylon and monofilament polyester screen fabrics are also classified according to thread diameter with the letters S, M, T or HD after the fabric number—S indicates the thread as thin, M as medium, T as a heavier diameter thread and HD as extra-heavy quality. Thus, a thinner ink deposit can be obtained with an S quality fabric than with the same numbered thread in an HD quality fabric. Different gauze thicknesses may be available for each numbered fabric. Type T fabric is commonly used; type HD offers longer life for printing large areas. Nylon and polyester are available in white, orange-red and red. The colors tend to protect against detrimental light scattering or undercutting in the exposure of direct emulsion-coated screens. Figure 43A presents a detailed print made with a screen coated with a direct emulsion on 6XX polyester (74 threads per inch; 29 threads per cm).

While each film or emulsion manufacturer may specify the method of cleaning off or degreasing the screen fabrics, usually silk is washed well in warm water and soap, rinsed thoroughly and dried before a coating or film is applied to it. Some printers clean other fabrics by scrubbing them carefully with kitchen type cleansers that contain a microscopic-type abrasive. However, as the printer must be careful not to weaken the threads, it is more practical to use an abrasive powder or paste recommended especially for the purpose. Other screen printers use a solution of warm water and trisodium phosphate, scrubbing the fabric with a nylon-type brush. The fabric should be rinsed thoroughly with water and dried before applying the film or coating. There are other methods of cleaning and preparing fabrics, each depending on the type of fabric and on the film or emulsion being applied. Some of these methods are covered in Chapter VIII.

*A micron is a one-millionth part of a meter.

66

Figure 43A. **A print made from a screen which was coated directly on a multifilament 6XX polyester fabric and exposed for 90 seconds to a 5000-watt pulsed xenon lamp that was 4 feet away.**

Photographic Printing Screens

Photographic printing screens are the most often used for commercial textile printing, because they reproduce any type of subject, effect or detail, and they are tough screens which will last for thousands of impressions. There are photographic screens which will print 50,000 impressions from one screen. Photographic-screen films and emulsions are similar to those used for general screen printing and are as simple to prepare. Some photographic screens have been developed specifically for use in textile printing. Although there are suppliers that will make any type of photographic screen for the textile printer, the printer is often forced to make his own screens in order to better control his process and to offer better service to his clients.

While photographic screens may be classified in various ways, there are three general types: (1) direct, (2) direct-indirect and (3) the indirect or transfer type. The direct screen is prepared by coating a photographic emulsion directly onto the screen fabric. A photographic positive containing the design is placed in direct contact with the underside of the emulsion-coated and dried screen. The screen is exposed through the positive side to a light source which hardens the exposed parts. Those parts on the positive not exposed or protected by the opaque areas, are

67

easily washed away with water, leaving areas open in the screen. The open areas represent the printing pattern.

The indirect or transfer-type screen-printing film is prepared first on a temporary support (usually a transparent thin plastic sheet). The processed film containing the design to be printed is then transferred and adhered to the underside of the prepared and cleaned screen fabric.

A direct-indirect or direct-film screen consists of an unsensitized dry film that is adhered semi-permanently to a paper or plastic support. The film is adhered to the underside of the screen by placing the screen fabric in direct and complete contact with the emulsion side of the film. A sensitized emulsion is then squeegeed onto the inside of the screen fabric over the film area. The emulsion sensitizes and adheres the film to the screen fabric. After the film dries, it is processed directly on the screen. There are also direct film products known as capillary films which may be adhered to the screen fabrics with water.

Some printers still prepare their screens with emulsions prepared in their own shops. However, with the very practical direct-coating emulsions available commercially and the techniques developed for protecting the emulsion and film from the varied dye pastes, the need for preparing one's own emulsion is lessened. It is best, especially for the beginner, to eliminate as much of the preparation as possible, because fewer steps diminish the chance of mistakes and carelessness in the screen preparation.

Any of these screens may be used for textile printing, depending on the job being produced, but direct screens are used most often commercially. The next chapter deals specifically with the preparation of direct printing screens*.

---

*The various types of photographic screens are treated more completely in the book: Kosloff, Albert. *Photographic Screen Printing*, Signs of the Times Publishing Co., Cincinnati, Ohio.

Chapter VIII

DIRECT PRINTING SCREENS FOR TEXTILE PRINTING

Screen-printing on textile materials makes exacting demands on the printing screens. The screen in textile printing, especially in machine printing, must last for thousands of impressions; in short-volume printing the screen may need to be saved, and cleaned again and again for reuse. After printing, it should be possible to reclaim or decoat the screen fabric without destroying it. The screen must resist alkali and acid pastes, vat dyes, oil-vehicle inks, water-soluble dyes, the various solvents and cleaning agents used and the elements in storage. The printing screen must be tough, resilient, durable and resistant to the abrasion action of the squeegee. If the screens are made locally in the shop, they must be easy to prepare without complex equipment. A variety of films and emulsion coatings must adhere to the screen fabrics used in the trade.

The prepared screen should print fine detail, halftone and large-area copy, and at the same time should not develop pinholes during the printing operation. The printing screen should allow some exposure latitude, and the products used in its preparation should not be too costly. The screens used for textile printing are generally of large or medium size, making it more difficult to stretch the fabric tight.

These requirements have been met, and processing has been standardized somewhat with the direct emulsions available. However, the printer must be completely familiar with the materials and equipment used. He should attempt small trial screens before making large commercial screens for volume printing, because reclaiming may not be possible if there are processing errors.

Since direct-printing screens are used most often for textile printing throughout the world, we shall deal with them first. As noted earlier, a direct-printing screen is a photographic screen-printing plate that is

69

prepared by directly coating the screen fabric with a light-sensitive emulsion. The coated, sensitized, dry screen, in direct contact with a transparent positive, is exposed to light, developed or washed-out, dried, and then used for printing. These steps involve a screen, an emulsion coating, a method of applying and processing the emulsion and some equipment.

The Screen

Regardless of the type of screen fabric on the screen, it must be stretched tight and be perfectly clean before applying emulsion or film to it. Wetting nylon before stretching and attaching it to the frame is helpful. The fabric must be tightly stretched to eliminate blurred printing, irregularities in registering colors, to eliminate wear and tear on the screen because of slackness and to ensure better adhesion of the film or coating. Some printers use a yellow nylon mesh which gives the screen some light transmission qualities, and tends to diminish the bouncing of the light between threads during exposure. Usually the fabric is tacked, stapled, or held to the screen frames with special fastening devices. The large printing screens employed for textile printing however, consist of special frames with stretching devices on them (see Figure 45), or are stretched on tensioning machines which have been developed specifically for stretching any mesh onto wood, aluminum or other metal frames. Figure 44 illustrates a four-floating bar frame which is used for many size screens and which stretches the fabrics tightly. The screen units

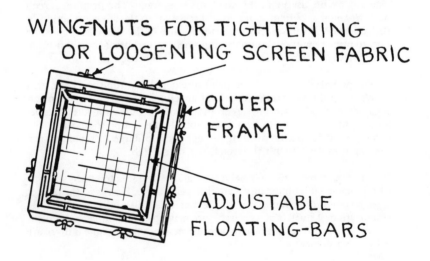

WING-NUTS FOR TIGHTENING
OR LOOSENING SCREEN FABRIC

OUTER
FRAME

ADJUSTABLE
FLOATING-BARS

Figure 44. **A wood four-floating bar frame.**

shown in Figures 47 and 48 illustrate the commercial types used for stretching and attaching fabrics. These and other types of screens are available in a variety of sizes for hand, semi-automatic and automatic printing.

After the fabric is stretched and attached, it must be thoroughly cleaned so that the film or coating will adhere to it. The cleaning procedure used depends on the type of fabric and on the type of emulsion or film. Silk of the multifilament-type usually presents no problems when adhering coatings and films to it. As has been explained, it is usually washed with warm water (about 110 degrees Fahrenheit; 43 degrees Celsius) and soap (or detergent). The soap must be rinsed off thoroughly with water so that it will not interfere with the processing. The fabric must be dried before the emulsion is applied to it.

There are a variety of methods for cleaning and degreasing nylon, polyester and metal cloth, and the proper one should be recommended by the manufacturer of the screen fabric or photographic emulsion and film. There are powders, degreasing solutions and pastes, microscopic abrasive compounds and special commercial liquid detergent cleansers available for new and used screen fabrics, that ensure the perfect and positive adherance of the films or emulsions.

The following are some of the methods that have been used to clean and degrease nylon fabric: (1) a caustic soda and scouring powder treatment—this consists of using a fifteen percent caustic soda solution (sodium hydroxide), and applying it well with a nylon brush, to both sides of the fabric for about twenty minutes. Because the solution is caustic, the processor should wear rubber gloves during this operation. After the solution is applied, the nylon is remoistened with water, and a sufficient quantity of a pumice-type kitchen cleanser is scrubbed over both sides of it. After scrubbing, the screen fabric is rinsed thoroughly with water, making sure that all traces of soda and powder are gone. (2) Tri-sodium phosphate—in this method the nylon is first scrubbed with an abrasive kitchen cleanser. The cleanser is washed off completely with water, and the tri-sodium powder is sprinkled on both sides of the nylon until the powder is dissolved. The powder is then washed off the mesh thoroughly with water. (3) Another cleansing method consists of using five cubic centimeters of sulphuric acid (66 degrees Be), and one-half gram of sodium or potassium bichromate dissolved in one liter of water. The solution is applied to the nylon and allowed to react for ten minutes. It is then rinsed off completely with water and dried before using.

Metal cloth, which is usually made of stainless steel threads (but may also be phosphor bronze or copper), must be thoroughly cleaned to remove its protective oil coating and any grease or finger marks, before coatings or films will adhere to it. This may be done by using commercial degreasing or cleaning solutions and mild abrasives available from

71

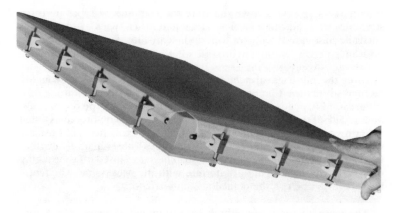

Figure 45. The Micro Frame Chase screen-frame unit available in any size for stretching any screen fabric drum tight. The fabric is tightened by attaching the hem binding to the four edges of the screen fabric, inserting rods through the hems and pulling them by uniformly tightening the special bolt fixtures. (Courtesy of Precision Screen Machines, Inc., Hawthorne, NJ)

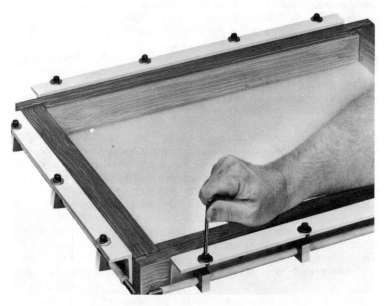

Figure 46. The Micro Frame Moulding which can be attached to any size wooden frame and is used for adding strength and for stretching any fabric. The screws at the top of the frame control the register and stretching even if the frame is in a printing machine or a master frame. (Courtesy of Precision Screen Machines, Inc., Hawthorne, NJ)

the suppliers, or by employing a five to ten percent acetic acid solution, scrubbing the solution onto the metal cloth with a brush for five minutes, and then rinsing well with hot water. The wire cloth may also be cleaned with a ten percent sodium hydroxide solution and rinsed off thoroughly with water. Applying a direct gas flame from a Bunsen burner *without burning the metal* will also clean the cloth. The cleaned fabric must not be touched in the areas that are to be covered with the coatings or film.

It must be stressed again that metal cloth, nylon and polyester should be prepared to have "tooth"—so that the films and coatings will adhere well to the threads; otherwise, the most superior films and emulsions will quickly wear away when printing. Also, when using any cleaning or other solution, it is suggested that the printer use rubber or protective gloves, especially if he is not familiar with the product.

Although it is recommended that nylon be stretched onto the frame when wet, this is not necessary with polyester fabric. Polyester may be degreased or cleaned with a caustic soda in a similar fashion to that used with nylon. After the solution remains on the fabric for fifteen minutes, it must be thoroughly rinsed off with water. The rinsed fabric should then be neutralized with a five percent acetic acid solution or a household white vinegar to ensure that the caustic soda solution does not remain on the fabric to react with the emulsion. The fabric should then be given a final water rinse.

Finally, it is probably more practical for the novice to purchase commercial cleaning and degreasing solutions, because often the manufacturer of a film or emulsion will suggest ways of preparing the fabric for receiving the emulsion coating or screen-printing film.

Assuming that the screen is now completely clean and ready for coating, the processor will need the following before starting to process a printing screen: (1) a photographic or hand-prepared positive with the design to be reproduced; (2) an emulsion coater, squeegee or sharp-edged piece of cardboard for applying the emulsion; (3) a commercial vacuum frame, photographic contact frame or other arrangement for exposing the coated screen; (4) an actinic light source for exposing the screen; (5) a darkroom or dark area; (6) a sink with a mixing faucet arrangement of hot and cold running water; (7) an electric fan; (8) a time clock or any clock with a second and minute hand for timing the exposure; (9) some soft cloths; (10) newsprint paper; (11) a photographic thermometer; and (12) an emulsion for coating the prepared screen.

Emulsions for Coating Screens

Screen-printing coating emulsions, available in both sensitized and unsensitized form, are viscous, adhesive solutions consisting of finely divided particles dispersed uniformly in a liquid in which they are suspended without dissolving. The emulsions, also known as colloidal suspensions, may consist of natural substances such as gelatin or glue, synthetic products such as polyvinyl alcohol or polyvinyl chloride, or combinations of these. Some of the emulsions also contain transparent dyes and inert powders. The sensitizers, substances or solutions mixed with the emulsions to make them light-sensitive are usually bichromate salts or solutions of potassium bichromate, ammonium bichromate, sodium bichromate or diazo-type sensitizers. The diazo sensitizers give the sensitized emulsions somewhat different properties than the bichromates, and are being used more often. There are some emulsions available, which when processed correctly, will resist most of the inks used in screen printing.

Generally, the emulsions are applied in their sensitized state to the screen fabric. There are unsensitized coatings which are applied to the screen fabric and dried. The sensitizer is then brushed quickly on both sides of the screen. The advantage of post-sensitizing is that the unsensitized coated screen can be stored for longer periods of time, and many screens can be coated at one time. There are other commercial presensitized direct emulsions that can be coated onto the screen fabric. After the screen dries, it may be stored for several weeks in complete darkness or shipped in black envelopes to other parts of the world. When the screen in received, it can be exposed, washed-out and used for printing. However, coated presensitized, unexposed screens do have time-limits for their storage.

Normally, screens which have been coated with bichromate-sensitized emulsions or films are not stored, but are exposed on the same day they are coated. However, diazo-sensitized screens may be stored for about three months in complete darkness, depending on the product used before exposure. The ability to store screens allows the textile printer to coat many screens at the same time, store them and use them as needed. Before coating and storing the screens, it is suggested that the printer test for the length of time it is safe to store them.

If the emulsion is unsensitized, a sensitizer is added to it. The sensitizer may be in a solution or powder form. Each sensitizer is different, depending on the type of emulsion to which it is added; each manufacturer recommends the specific sensitizer to be used or furnishes the sensitizer in a ready-to-use form. Through the years, this writer has had the privilege to test dozens of emulsions from the various manufacturers, and has found almost all of them to be practical, if the manufacturer's directions are followed. Often the emulsion was developed by an enterprising printer in answer to a specific need; after much testing, it was found that the formulation could be used to print on a variety of surfaces and materials. Instructions for the preparation of sensitized emulsions are simple.

Sensitizers can be stored if kept in a dark brown glass container in a dark, cool place. It is best to dissolve the sensitizer powder in distilled water if water is suggested, and use the sensitizing solution as needed. Generally, unsensitized emulsions can be stored for long periods of time, if they are stored in tightly covered containers under normal atmospheric conditions. The writer prefers to keep most of the solutions in polyethylene containers, using a different shaped container for the sensitizer than for the emulsion. Each solution must be clearly labeled. Some solutions may be harmful to the skin; in such cases it is suggested that the printer wear rubber or other type protective gloves.

Usually the sensitizer is added to the emulsion, and stirred in the same direction with a glass rod until the two solutions are thoroughly mixed. If there are air bubbles in the mixture it should be strained through a piece of screen fabric before using. Formulas are mixed in proportions according to units of weight or volume, depending on the manufacturer. The following are formulas presented for the printer who may desire to mix direct emulsions. He may use metric or U.S. units for mixing.

(A) Add 28 parts by weight of gelatin to 100 parts by weight of water; when the gelatin is completely dissolved, add 3 1/2 parts by weight of potassium bichromate powder to the gelatin solution.
   Note—The gelatin used is usually photographic gelatin.

(B) Dissolve fifteen parts by weight of gelatin in 50 parts by weight of water; mix one part by weight of zirconium oxide in three parts of water, and add the zirconium oxide mixture to the gelatin solution; then add 31 parts of a fifteen percent ammonium bichromate solution to the gelatin-zirconium oxide solution.

(C) Dissolve slowly 95 parts by weight of a fine polyvinyl alcohol powder in 75 parts by weight of water that is 140 to 160 degrees Fahrenheit (60 to 71 degrees Celsius); to this polyvinyl alcohol solution add a sensitizing solution that is made by dissolving six parts by weight of ammonium bichromate in 25 parts by weight of water. A drop of inert dye or powder may be added to the mixture as an aid in developing or washing-out the screen.

(D) Dissolve completely four parts by weight of polyvinyl alcohol in 40 parts by weight of water; then add one part by weight of ammonium bichromate or potassium bichromate powder and a few drops of inert dye, such as green stamp pad ink.

(E) Make up three solutions—solution (1) is made by adding one part by weight of dibutyl phthalate to eleven parts by weight of a polyvinyl acetate solution; solution (2) is made by dissolving one part by weight of polyvinyl alcohol in four parts by weight of water; and solution (3) is a sensitizing solution made by dissolving eighteen parts by weight of ammonium or potassium bichromate powder in 82 parts by weight of water. To prepare the coating emulsion, add five parts by weight of the polyvinyl acetate-dibutyl phthalate solution, and when these are well mixed add six parts by weight of the sensitizing solution.*

Coating Screens

The direct emulsions available ordinarily do not require a darkroom for application and may be applied under a subdued light (such as a fifteen-watt incandescent bulb) with special coaters, squeegees or a sharp-edged piece of cardboard. Figure 47 presents one type of emulsion coater. The emulsion may be applied either on the underside, or on both sides of the screen, applying the first coat on the inside of the screen and the second and third coats on the underside. All of the coats may also be applied on the underside of the screen, as this has a tendency to produce sharper printing and eliminates serrated or ragged edges when printing fine detail. Although two coats may suffice for general screen printing, as many as five coats may need to be applied on textile screens, the first coat being applied to the inside, and the rest of the coats to the underside or outside of the screen fabric.

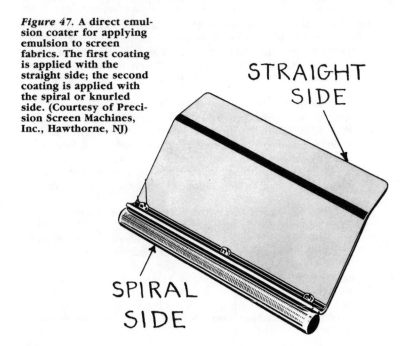

Figure 47. **A direct emulsion coater for applying emulsion to screen fabrics. The first coating is applied with the straight side; the second coating is applied with the spiral or knurled side. (Courtesy of Precision Screen Machines, Inc., Hawthorne, NJ)**

STRAIGHT
SIDE

SPIRAL
SIDE

To coat the screen, pour some emulsion on the underside of the screen at one edge and squeegee the coating once or twice, back and forth, applying the solution evenly until all of the fabric is covered. The coater or squeegee should be about two inches shorter than the inside dimensions of the width of the screen frame. If there is too much coating on the inside of the screen, scrape the coater once across the inside. Wipe away the excess solution along the frame, and allow the coated fabric to dry in a horizontal position in complete darkness. While emulsions are not light-sensitive in solution form, the coating becomes sensitive as it dries.

A fan may be used to dry the applied coating; usually most coatings should not be dried with heat. The first coat should not be too thick. After the first coat has dried, a second coat is applied on the underside of the screen in a similar fashion and dried completely in the dark. As mentioned earlier, for most work, two well-applied coats will suffice. However, for a tough screen, needed for thousands of impressions, it may be necessary to apply more coats. The screen must be kept in complete darkness after it is dry, and with most direct emulsions it should be exposed immediately or within one to two hours. If the dried screen is stored for longer periods, it should be done only upon the recommendation of the manufacturer or the results of objective trials.

Sometimes a very large screen is coated with emulsion only in the design areas of the screen. A smaller area is easier to apply and requires the use of a shorter emulsion coater. The open areas of the screen outside the design area, are filled in with emulsion after the printing screen has been completely processed.

Another common method of coating is to apply the emulsion with a coating trough or even a squeegee, coating the underside of the screen fabric twice and applying the second coat while the first is still wet. Then while the coating is still wet, apply wet coat to the inside of the screen once, pushing the emulsion through to the underside.

The coats may be allowed to dry naturally or with the aid of a fan, preferably with the coated side of the screen down.

When printing detail and halftones, there may be no need for repeat coatings. However, for heavy print deposits and maximum durability, repeat coatings should be applied on the inside of the screen mesh and on the underside of the screen once or twice, allowing the coated screen to dry completely in the dark.

Exposing Screen to Light

The screen is exposed in direct contact with the positive, as shown in Figure 48. The photographic contact unit illustrated in Figure 48 may

77

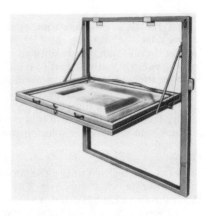

Figure 49. **A space-saving wall model Douthitt Direct Method Vacuum Frame used for exposing direct, direct-indirect and indirect printing screens in any size up to 73" x 72" (185cm x 183cm) in area. The screen is placed in the unit in a horizontal position and is tilted into a vertical position for exposure. (Courtesy of The Douthitt Corporation, Detroit, MI)**

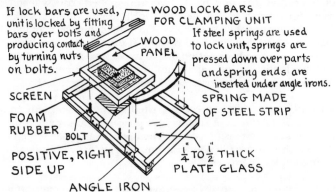

If lock bars are used, unit is locked by fitting bars over bolts and producing contact by turning nuts on bolts.

WOOD LOCK BARS FOR CLAMPING UNIT

WOOD PANEL

If steel springs are used to lock unit, springs are pressed down over parts and spring ends are inserted under angle irons.

SCREEN

FOAM RUBBER

BOLT

SPRING MADE OF STEEL STRIP

POSITIVE, RIGHT SIDE UP

$\frac{1}{4}$" TO $\frac{1}{2}$" THICK PLATE GLASS

ANGLE IRON

Figure 48. **A photographic contact frame that may be used for exposing direct screens and screen-process films. Either one of the two methods shown may be used for locking parts of the frame.**

be used to expose small and medium-sized screens. Also, the printer has his choice of using wood lock-bars or steel springs to clamp the parts together in perfect contact. The printer may make this unit or have it made for him. Pulsed-xenon lamps, carbon arc lamps (see Figures 56 and 57), blacklight fluorescent units, mercury vapor lamps, photoflood lamps or good sunlight may be used to expose direct screens. Actinic light, to which the screen is exposed, consists of light rays that are capable of changing a photographic material when the light strikes it. Regardless of the type of light used, the light should produce a uniform chemical change in all exposed areas during the time of exposure.

The exposure time depends on the type of emulsion used, the type of light used and the distance of the screen from the light source. For example, for arc lights the distance may be 2 1/2 to four feet; for blacklight tubes the distance may be about four inches. The time of ex-

78

Figure 50. The Douthitt vacuum frame in a closed position with the vacuum on and the blanket maintaining a vacuum contact over the screen. (Courtesy of Douthitt Corporation, Detroit, MI)

posure may vary from about 1 1/2 to fifteen minutes. If the beginner does not know the time of exposure, he may easily determine it by pasting strips of opaque tape on top of the glass over the positive, placing the one tape strip next to the other, until the entire positive area is covered. When the exposure is started, the processor will peel off one strip of tape the first half-minute, the second strip after one minute, etc., until all the strips have been peeled off at equal time intervals. Some parts of the screen will have been underexposed and some overexposed. The exposures must be done at the same distance from the light source. When the exposed screen is developed, the best image will be evident, making the best time-range obvious.

Commercial contact vacuum frames are the most practical and the best units for the exposure of screens and films (see Figures 49, 50 and 51), but when not available, the "cement method" (or even the use of grease) may be employed. Although smaller and medium-sized screens are used for this method, it is the size of the film positive that governs the application of the cementing positive to the screen fabric. One must make sure that larger positives are in complete contact with the screen fabric. A good quality rubber cement, consisting of one part cement and one part cement solvent or benzol, is used in the cement method. The cement is brushed carefully over the film positive side, which is to come into contact with the fabric, and over the area of the screen fabric that is to contact the positive. When the cement is dry (it dries quickly), the cement-covered positive is placed, cement side up, on a flat smooth surface, and the screen is placed over the positive so that both cement-covered surfaces are in contact. Then the processor rolls a rubber roller or brayer on the inside of the screen over the positive so that every spot on the positive is in contact with the screen fabric.

Another way to adhere the positive is to place two sheets of newsprint paper on the inside of the screen, rubbing the top of the paper with a soft cloth to obtain complete contact between the positive and the screen. The screen is then exposed. After exposure, the positive is peeled off, the cement is rubbed off quickly with one's finger or with a soft cloth dipped in cement solvent and the screen is washed-out. A quick way to remove rubber cement from the screen is to attach masking tape to a rubber roller so that the sticky side of the tape is on the outside of the roller, and roll carefully over the cement area. The cement will stick to the tape.

A light-colored grease may be used instead of cement. The process is similar except that the grease is applied on the bottom surface of the screen with a squeegee. The screen is placed over the positive, as with the cement. The closer the contact of the positive to the screen, the better the exposure. The grease may be cleaned off with a cloth dipped in the correct solvent.

As shown in the various illustrations, a variety of devices and techniques for exposing screens and screen-printing films have been and are being used by screen printers.

Figure 51. The Cooper Graphics Vacuum Exposure Unit consists of a flexible plastic envelope and a vacuum pump device for exposing areas up to 54″ by 120″ (137cm x 305cm). The item to be exposed is inserted in the envelope and the air in the envelope is evacuated, producing contact between the positive and the screen. The unit is portable and may be exposed in a horizontal or vertical position. (Courtesy of Cooper Graphics, Niagra Falls, NY)

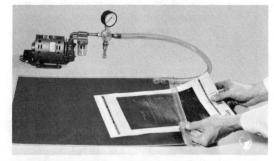

Washing-Out

The exposed screen should be washed-out in water immediately after exposure. After both sides of the screen have been wetted in water, the lights may be turned on, since the light sensitivity of the screen is greatly reduced when it is wet. Some coatings require warm water, (although not warmer than 115 degrees Fahrenheit; 46 degrees Celsius) and some may be washed in cold water. Usually the washing-out is done by spraying water onto the screen, first on the underside and then on the inside. Those parts of the screen which were not exposed or were protected by the opaque parts of the positive will wash away easily, if the screen was coated and exposed correctly. After the screen is dried (drying may be hastened with the aid of a fan), it can be prepared for printing.

Reclaiming or Decoating Film Screens

The same qualities that make emulsions resistant to inks and solvents also make them more difficult to remove from the screen fabric. It is

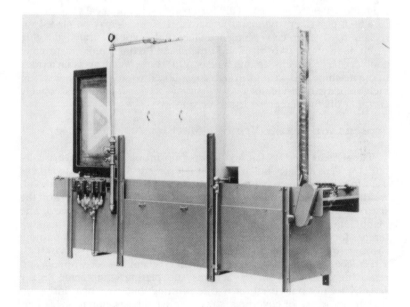

Figure 52. **A completely automatic machine which cleans, washes and removes emulsions, sludge and contaminants from any size screen. (Courtesy of M and M Research, Oshkosh, Wisconsin)**

81

suggested that the printer attempt to reclaim a small screen before decoating the very large screens used for textile printing. Different emulsions are removed with different types of reclaiming solutions or agents. The manufacturer of the emulsion will specify the most practical method for reclaiming the screen, when this is necessary. Gelatin coatings without hardening agents or enamels can be removed with enzyme-type removers available from screen suppliers. Generally, metal and nylon fabrics can be reclaimed; it is more difficult with silk because the techniques or solvents that will remove the emulsions may also damage the silk.

Before reclaiming the screen, it is essential that the dye paste is cleaned off thoroughly immediately after printing so that none of the dye paste dries into the fabric. This may be accomplished with commercial screen-cleaning units or by hand-cleaning. If the emulsion or film coating has not had an enamel or hardening agent applied over it, it may be removed. If reclaiming powders or solutions are used, they must be washed away completely. Any trace of solution that remains on the fabric may prevent future films or coatings from adhering properly.

Shops that reclaim many screens each day usually use screen- reclaiming tanks and varied automatic screen-washing machines. The reclaiming tanks are filled with specially formulated safe chemical solutions into which polyester, nylon and metal fabric screens may be placed for reclaiming. The screen-washing machines of the type illustrated in Figure 52 come in a variety of sizes and designs, and will accommodate small and very large screens. In this type of unit, the screen travels on a track in the machine and passes through an enclosed washing chamber where high-velocity, high-volume nozzles spray water or solutions, effectively cleaning off the screen so it can be reused.

Screens for Textile-Printing Machines

The screens used for flat textile screen-printing machines are usually direct screens and are similar to other flat screens. However, the screens used for rotary screen-printing machines consist of round, cylindrical, weldless light-weight metal (often nickel), vary in size depending on the size of the repeat pattern to be printed and are precision-processed. The manufacturer of the rotary machine may offer the service of making screens for the textile shop or mill. However, large textile screen-printing shops or mills will usually have special equipment, screens, materials, screen-coating equipment, drying chambers, chemicals for stripping and removing coatings from the screens and plating equipment. Rotary screens are not only used for textile printing, but also for printing on transfer paper, floor coverings, paper, wallcoverings, imitation leather, circuit printing, etc.

The rotary screens, which are specifically made for each machine, have an equal thickness across their entire printing width, and are available in a variety of meshes which may be reordered when necessary. While some cylindrical screens may be plated or electroformed, generally, the round screens used have minutely perforated holes in the metal which may be varied in the mesh. The size of the screen may vary from about 790mm (31.6″) to 2800mm (112″), and the screens are designed to print repeats that vary from about 48cm to 183cm (19″ to 72″) and in mesh sizes that may vary from about nine to 100 per cm (23 to 250 per inch).

While many types of emulsions are available for flat and rotary screens, there are direct emulsions formulated especially for metal rotary printing screens that have perforations in their cylinders. Ordinarily, the first emulsion or lacquer coat applied will be a thinner coat, applied to a thoroughly cleaned and degreased cylindrical screen. Two or three additional coats may be applied over the first coat, each drying at 70 to 85 degrees Fahrenheit (20 to 30 degrees Celsius) for about fifteen minutes. The light-sensitive emulsion may be applied over the metal screen mechanically or manually by moving a circular squeegee device around the screen from top to bottom. After the coatings on the screen dry, a photographic film bearing the design is stretched around the screen so that the film and the screen are in complete contact with one another. The screen is then exposed in a special exposure machine. After exposure, the screen is developed with a developing solution. The emulsion is then cured at 350 to 675 degrees Fahrenheit (180 to 356 degrees Celsius). The screens may be reclaimed after printing, by being placed horizontally in a stripping tank which contains a special solution that removes the hardened emulsion or photographic coating from the screen without attacking it.

Figure 52A. A detailed design printed on cotton handkerchiefs with a red water-based textile screen-printing ink, using a direct-printing screen for printing the pattern.

Chapter IX

TRANSFER OR INDIRECT-TYPE PRINTING SCREENS FOR TEXTILE PRINTING

Although today, modern direct printing screens and direct-indirect screens are used most often in textile printing, indirect or transfer- type screen-printing films are also sometimes used. Originally films and carbon-tissue screens were used for textile printing, and some screen-printing films were developed specifically for printing on textiles before direct and direct-indirect products were practical and commercially available. Films and carbon tissue intended for long runs were and are treated with a toughening agent to aid in resisting the negative effects of textile dyes and inks.

The indirect or transfer-type printing screen employed for printing on textile surfaces is similar to that used for general printing. Transfer or indirect printing screens may be prepared from various commercial screen-printing films or from carbon tissue. In this type of screen, the film or coating is first prepared on a support and then the processed film containing the design or image is transferred and adhered to the underside of the screen fabric. There are available paper-backed carbon tissues and varied screen-printing films on thin transparent plastic-backed sheets, the sheets serving as the support in processing and holding the emulsion. Screen-printing films may be processed under subdued light and do not require a darkroom with complex equipment. Films may be adhered to silk, synthetic fabrics and metal fabrics. All film products should be stored, handled and processed as recommended by the manufacturer of each specific product.

Generally, there are two types of screen-printing films: (1) unsensitized—those which have to be sensitized by the printer and (2) pre-sensitized—those which do not have to be sensitized by the printer. Among the unsensitized films are a variety of commercial screen-printing films, usually coated on a thin transparent plastic sheet or carbon tissue

84

(pigment paper or photo-stencil paper). Carbon tissue, which was the first product used commercially for transfer or indirect screens, is a photographic material that consists of an absorbent acid-free strong paper onto which is coated a photographic gelatin composition with coloring agents such as pigments or dyes and plasticizers. In the 1920s when it was first being introduced to the screen-printing trade, a printer adapted the tissue which was and is still being used in gravure printing as a resist on printing cylinders. Today's carbon tissue, both in the United States and abroad, is manufactured specifically for the screen-printing trade.

Because screen-printing films are based on the same principles as carbon tissue products, the processing of carbon tissue is presented to show the relationship of this printing screen to unsensitized screen- printing films (which developed from it), and also to present an economical screen that is available today in various parts of the world. Screen-printing films are available in any width that the printer may need and in rolls up to about 100 feet in length.

While the procedure in processing screen-printing films and carbon tissue is simple, the steps must be carried out exactly as specified in the directions for each product, and should be standardized. The procedure consists of sensitizing the film or the carbon tissue if the product is in an unsensitized form, exposing the sensitized film to an actinic light, washing-out or developing, and adhering the washed-out image to the screen fabric.

Presensitized films do not have to be sensitized and are exposed dry. Many sensitized screen-printing films are exposed when the films are wet or damp. There are two general methods of exposing carbon tissue: the ''wet-exposure'' and the ''dry-exposure'' method. In the dry method the carbon tissue is dried in the dark after it is sensitized, and then exposed to light when it is dry; in the wet method, the carbon tissue is sensitized and exposed to light while it is damp. While there are advantages and disadvantages to both methods, the wet method is more frequently used.

Preparing Screen Fabric

The preparation of the screen fabric, as that for direct screens, must be done accurately. With indirect screens, the film adheres to the underside of the screen fabric, while with the application of direct emulsions the coating usually impregnates the fabric. Therefore, the printer must make sure that the fabric is sterile and clean, and is prepared in a similar fashion to that explained in Chapter VIII for the application of direct emulsions. While films and carbon tissues adhere best to silk because of the nature and properties of its multifilament fibers, they will also adhere to the synthetic and metal cloths available in the trade. The screen fabric must be tightly stretched and must remain stretched tight once the film is adhered. While film is used more often for detailed printing, with screen fabrics ranging from No. 10 through No. 18 good quality mesh being used for photographic screens, coarser and finer weaves of fabric may also be employed. If a fabric that has been reclaimed or decoated is used, the printer must make sure that the mesh does not contain any trace of the decoating composition; when the wet film is attached, any decoating compound or enzyme that remains on the fabric will prevent the film from adhering well to the mesh and will wear off quickly in printing.

Sensitizing

Presensitized commercial products can be exposed without first being sensitized. Unsensitized screen-printing films and carbon tissue must be sensitized before exposure. The sensitizing solution for carbon tissue is made by dissolving photographic or chemical powders, or granules of potassium bichromate, ammonium bichromate or sodium bichromate, in a given amount of water. The first two bichromates are most often used for sensitizing solutions. Usually the bichromate is dissolved just in water. Additives should not be included in the sensitizers unless they are recommended by the manufacturer of the specific film. The bichromate sensitizing solution can be kept for long periods of time, in a dark brown glass container in a cool place under ordinary atmospheric conditions. When used, the sensitizing solutions should be about 60 degrees Fahrenheit (16 degrees Celsius) or colder. The solution may be kept and cooled in an ordinary household refrigerator before use.

For sensitizing carbon tissue, two to three percent bichromate solutions are used. (A two percent solution is made by dissolving two percent by weight of the powder in 98 percent by weight of water.) If there is doubt about the cleanliness of the water, it is best to use distilled water. Some commercial films have different sensitizers or different proportions of bichromate solutions and may specify the addition of one or two additives. For example, to sensitize carbon tissue, insert the tissue, emulsion side up, for two to three minutes in a tray that contains the cool bichromate solution, rubbing the sensitizer solution over the emulsion side with one's hand or with a rubber glove. Make sure that all the emulsion has been soaked in the sensitizing solution. The sensitized tissue is then positioned, emulsion side down, on a thin transparent plastic sheet (.002 inch to .005 inch thick transparent polyester or vinyl plastic which has been wetted with the sensitizer). The tissue is then squeegeed onto the plastic support sheet, from the center outward, making sure that no air is trapped between the support and the tissue. The excess sensitizer on top of the paper and on the plastic sheet should be wiped off before exposure. The "sandwich," consisting of the emulsion between the backing sheet and the transparent support, is then exposed as shown in Figure 53. Polyester and vinyl sheets are used, because the dry tissue will peel off easily from them; other types of supports have

86

to be waxed and polished before the tissue is squeegeed on.

Although the professional textile screen printer today may not use carbon tissue in his preparation of screens, it is an inexpensive product, and a good first screen for the novice, student or apprentice to prepare.

In addition to carbon tissues, there are emulsions on thin transparent plastic sheets which must also be sensitized before processing. These commercial screen-printing films are sensitized by: (1) immersing the film in a tray of sensitizing solution for a given period of time; (2) brushing the sensitizing solution on the emulsion side, first in a horizontal direction and then in a vertical direction, thereby ensuring that the gelatinous coating is saturated with solution; and (3) brushing the sensitizer on the emulsion side of the film and then placing the sensitized emulsion side of the film in contact with a piece of kraft paper, both sides of which have been thoroughly coated with sensitizer. If the screen-printing film needs to be dried, it must be dried and handled in complete darkness or under safelights. A fan can be used to hasten the drying.

Usually the sensitizing procedure for commercial films has specific instructions and is simple to perform. The sensitizers are available in pre-measured portions or containers, eliminating the possibility of the printer making mistakes in measuring. Commercial screen-printing films are usually coated on very thin transparent backing sheets or supports. Plastic supports do not expand or contract because of atmospheric changes as do paper backing sheets. The plastic backing sheet also serves as the support in processing and is usually exposed so that light hits it first, then the film (see Figure 54).

Commercial presensitized film eliminates this sensitizing step. All that

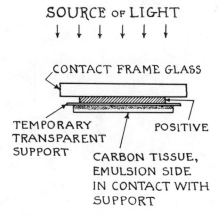

Figure 53. Exposing carbon tissue that is on a temporary transparent support in contact with the positive.

SOURCE OF LIGHT

↓ ↓ ↓ ↓ ↓ ↓

CONTACT FRAME GLASS

TEMPORARY TRANSPARENT SUPPORT

POSITIVE

CARBON TISSUE, EMULSION SIDE IN CONTACT WITH SUPPORT

is necessary is to cut the film so that it is slightly larger than the positive and then expose the film in contact with the positive.

Exposing

The purpose of exposing is to harden or chemically change the parts of the sensitized screen films or emulsions that are struck by light. The transparent positive governs which parts are to be hardened. Those parts which are to be left open in the printing screen and which are to print, are not hardened by light. Positives may be hand-drawn on transparent or translucent plastic sheets or on vellum-type paper; they may be hand-cut from knife-cut film; they may be photographic films; or they may consist of paste-up designs on transparent sheets. Regardless of the type, positives must have definite opaque and transparent areas on them. Commercial shops use process cameras of the type shown in Figure 55 to make the negatives, positives, autopositives, photographic enlargements and reductions and all the photographic work needed to produce screen printing. In addition to offering immediate photographic service to the shop in which it is needed, this type of equipment, in time, pays for itself in labor and time saved.

The prepared film is exposed in complete contact with the positive so that the light strikes the positive first, and then the film, (Figures 53 and 54). Pulsed-xenon lamps, carbon arc lamps, metal halide exposing units, fluorescent-tube units, mercury vapor lamps, the sun and photoflood lamps are all used for exposing. The first five light sources listed are the most practical and the most commonly used. Figures 56, 57 and 57A present three types of commercial lamps that may be used by the screen printer.

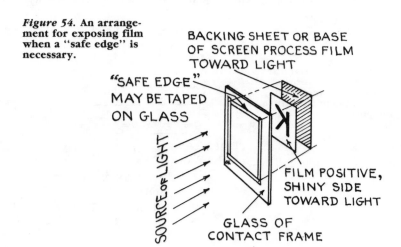

Figure 54. An arrangement for exposing film when a "safe edge" is necessary.

BACKING SHEET OR BASE OF SCREEN PROCESS FILM TOWARD LIGHT

"SAFE EDGE" MAY BE TAPED ON GLASS

SOURCE of LIGHT

FILM POSITIVE, SHINY SIDE TOWARD LIGHT

GLASS OF CONTACT FRAME

Figure 55. The nuArc darkroom horizontal camera, designed for the variety of photographic work that is done in screen-printing shops. It has the following specifications: a contact screen up to 21″ x 25″ (53cm x 63.5cm); a film size 20″ x 24″ (50.9cm x 61cm); copyboards 30″ x 40″ (76cm x 101.6cm); an 18″ (45.7cm) precision color-corrected lens that enlarges up to 300% (3X) and reduces down to 20% (5X); it uses six quartz iodine cycle lamps for lighting; and operates on 220 volts at 26 amperes. (Courtesy of nuArc Co., Inc, Chicago, IL)

When exposing carbon tissue products and gelatinous emulsions coated on paper backing sheets, the positive is placed on the contact frame glass so that the positive reads right side up; the carbon tissue which is on the temporary support is placed in contact with the positive; and the plastic sheet is placed in contact with the emulsion side of the positive, as illustrated in Figures 53 and 54. The printer must make sure that all moisture is wiped off, that there is complete contact between the tissue and the positive, and that the glass in the exposing unit is clean and has no dust particles on it. Dust or other minute particles can cause pinholes in the final printing screen. Then, opaque paper or tape is fastened on top of the glass along the four edges of the tissue, so that the tape overlaps and forms a margin of at least 1/4 inch width on all four edges of the tissue, as illustrated in Figure 54. The purpose of the opaque margin is to provide an unexposed edge or "safe edge" on the film or tissue, which will allow the backing paper to be easily removed when washing-out without damaging the film or the gelatinous coating.

As mentioned earlier, presensitized commercial screen-printing film generally comes on a transparent plastic thin backing sheet. The film

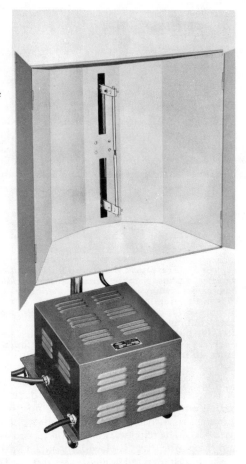

Figure 56. A nuArc single arc lamp that works automatically, producing constant light and color intensity for exposing screens, screen-printing films and other photographic products. (Courtesy of nuArc Company, Inc., Chicago, IL)

is exposed as illustrated in Figure 54, so that the backing sheet side of the film is in contact with the emulsion side of the positive (usually the emulsion side of the positive is dull; the backing sheet is shiny). The light strikes the positive first, then the transparent backing sheet, then the film on the backing sheet.

The time of exposure depends on the type of film, the distance of the light from the film, the type of light, the type of positive and the detail of the design to be reproduced. For example, a positive hand-drawn on translucent photographic vellum paper may be exposed 1/5 to 1/3 longer than a perfectly transparent photographic-film positive, all else being equal. On the other hand, a very fine detailed film positive, may require a shorter exposure time. The thickness and strength of the film

90

can be varied with the exposure and development or wash-out time. It is important that the printer find the best exposure time for his type of printing screens and equipment.

When the time and distance of exposure are not specified for a product, as there are varied types of exposing units and distances of exposure, the printer may determine the correct distance and time with a trial exposure in which he overexposes some parts of the film and underexposes other parts. As explained in the exposure of direct screens in Chapter VIII, this may be accomplished by taping strips of opaque tape on the contact frame glass over the film area, and peeling off a strip of tape at a time at equal time intervals. Typical exposures for films range in time from about ten seconds to about 25 minutes, at distances varying from about four inches for blacklight fluorescent-tube units to six feet for carbon arc lamps. The farther the light source is from the screen, the longer the time of exposure.

Figure 57. A nuArc new light printing lamp with two pulsed-xenon arc tube-lights, that has a constant color temperature of 6,000 degrees Kelvin which produces a point light source of 8,000-watts for coverage of large vacuum frames and other exposing. (Courtesy of nuArc Company, Inc., Chicago, IL)

Figure 57A. The Day Star II, a metal halide unit used for exposing sensitized printing screens, is equivalent to a 20 ampere carbon arc lamp, and has a scientifically designed reflector, practical for the smaller shop. (Courtesy of Naz-Dar Company, Chicago, IL)

Because wet carbon tissue and wet gelatinous films may melt at temperatures over 88 degrees Fahrenheit (31 degrees Celsius), it is suggested that a fan be used to blow over the tissue, if the light source used gives off much heat, the exposure is long and the atmosphere is humid and warm. This will help keep the gelatinous emulsion cool. Large shops have air-conditioned rooms and darkrooms where a lot of work is done, so that standard working conditions prevail.

Washing-Out or Developing Exposed Films

Generally, exposed film should be developed immediately. Many films and carbon tissues are washed-out and developed in water only; some films are supplied with special developing solutions specified by the manufacturer. If the image washes off too easily from the base, it may be underexposed. Gelatinous films and exposed carbon tissue are usually washed-out in warm water (110 to 115 degrees Fahrenheit; 43 to 46 degrees Celsius), either by gently spraying water on the film or by rocking the film in a tray of water. Because the gelatin on the exposed carbon tissue is between the backing paper and the transparent support (Figure 53), it is necessary to remove the backing paper before washing-out and developing. This is done by soaking the tissue on the support in warm water for about one minute or until the gelatin begins to ooze out from between the paper and the support. The backing paper is then stripped off and the image is carefully flooded with hot water until all the soluble gelatin is washed away and the image appears clean and sharp on the temporary support.

When the films require the mixing of special additives to the developing water, the powder or liquid additives should be added in specific proportions to the water before the film is placed in the developer. After several minutes, the film is washed off with warm and cold water and then adhered to the screen fabric. Additives, conversion powders or solutions, or activators (as they are often called) are used for better processing and to produce a stronger film. As some of these additives are toxic, they should be handled with rubber gloves and applied to the film or the film on the fabric with care.

Adhering Film to Fabric

When adhering any film to a screen fabric, the printer must be sure that he has complete contact between all parts of the processed film and the fabric. This can best be accomplished by using a perfectly flat built-up layer, as illustrated in Figure 41, which may be glass or any flat board about 3/8 inch thick, smaller in area than the inside dimensions of the screen frame, and larger than the film. The film is placed on the layer emulsion side up, the screen fabric is positioned over the film and pressed down squarely and firmly. Excess water may be blotted up with newsprint paper, using even pressure to ensure perfect adhesion of all parts of the film to the fabric, and being careful not to move the screen. Weights may be placed on the frame sides to keep the screen in contact with the film until the film dries and adheres to the mesh. This should take from several minutes to about twenty minutes depending on the film and atmospheric conditions. When the film is dry, the backing sheet or temporary support will peel off easily or will come off by itself.

Hardening or Making Films More Resistant

Although commercial films will last for very many impressions, and may be cleaned and used over and over if processed and used correctly, most gelatinous photographic films will not resist the acid and alkali dye pastes and solvents as well as they do the inks used in general screen printing. When it is necessary to print very long runs from one screen, textile printers apply reinforcing agents such as lacquers, alkyd synthetic enamels, varnishes and commercial coatings on the inside of the screen, or on both sides of the screen over the gelatinous emulsion. These reinforcing mediums may be used on all types of screen fabrics. Commercial coatings must be used exactly as recommended by the manufacturer.

The following solution may be used to give a hardening treatment to screens that are made of gelatin and sensitized with bichromates. This solution is made by dissolving one part by weight of ammonium bichromate crystals and two parts by weight of chrome alum crystals in two parts of a formaldehyde solution (40 percent solution). This hardening solution is brushed on both sides of the screen and left on for ten to fifteen minutes to react. The screen is then washed well in cold water and allowed to dry slowly.

Reinforcing is generally done on indirect gelatinous-film screens, but it may also be done on direct screens. The lacquer or enamel method of reinforcing may be used on all types of screens. The lacquer, enamel and varnish-coating methods of reinforcing screens consist of placing the screen so that the design to be printed is resting perfectly flat on an absorbent surface such as blotting paper or several layers of newsprint paper. The lacquer or finish which is to resist the dye paste is squeegeed well once or twice onto the inside of the screen so that the lacquer or enamel is absorbed through the design areas by the paper, and the rest of the reinforcing agent is left coated on the inside of the screen. Usually a thin deposit of the coating is desirable. The viscosity of the coating is similar to that of the screen inks generally used. The outside or underside of the screen may be rubbed carefully with a soft dry cloth to ensure the removal of any remaining traces from the open areas of the screen. When the finish dries it will offer a coating that resists the inks to be printed.

The large shops which specialize in textile screen preparation and textile printing may have a varnish-suction or reinforcing-suction machine for applying a protective finish over the film, as illustrated in Figure 58. This type of machine is usually designed so that various sized screens may be placed in a horizontal position over the unit which has a suction slot similar to that of a vacuum cleaner. As the suction slot is moved under the screen, it sucks or vacuums the reinforcing finish through the screen openings, leaving only the desired coating on the screen. Once the screen is placed horizontally on the machine frame that holds it, it may be shifted into any position over the suction slot. If necessary, after the coating dries on the inside of the screen, an enamel or medium may be applied on the underside of the screen. Sometimes two very thin coatings should be applied.

The negative (or reverse) method is another way of reinforcing textile screens. In this method, a negative instead of a photographic positive is used to expose the screen. After the exposed screen is washed-out, a hardening coat or a lacquer is applied to the entire underside of the screen with a squeegee or coating trough. After the coating is dry (or

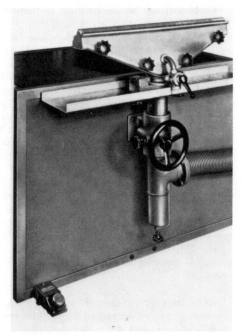

Figure 58. A varnish suction machine which makes possible the suction of the varied liquid reinforcing coatings from the printing screen in the pre- and after-reinforcing processes. (Courtesy of ABC Photo Supply Corporation, Paterson, NJ)

hardens), the emulsion can be removed from the screen with a lukewarm solution of bleach or another solvent. In removing the emulsion, the reinforcing coating will wash away, leaving a clean, sharp and open image or design. Before reinforcing large screens, it is suggested that the printer test his method on a small trial screen.

The same techniques and reinforcing agents may also be used to reinforce screens for printing with ceramic, plastic or any other ink that has a tendency to dissolve away the film or emulsion.

Reclaiming or Decoating Screens

Gelatinous films are usually easier to remove from screen fabrics than direct emulsions. To aid in the removal of films, the ink or dye paste should be cleaned off the screen thoroughly immediately after printing, to prevent the ink from drying into the mesh and over the film edges. Generally, for very long-run jobs, the screens are prepared and reinforced so that it is not practical to reclaim them. Films which have been coated with reinforcing mediums cannot be reclaimed unless the medium is dissolved away first. This can be done on metal screen fabrics, but not successfully on any other fabrics, because the solvent or method which removes the hardening agent may also damage the fabric.

95

Carbon tissue and gelatinous films may be removed with special reclaiming agents that are available in liquid or powder form, with enzyme-type reclaiming solutions and a variety of other techniques. Lactic acid swabbed (or brushed) on will soften the gelatinous film in a few minutes so that it will be soft enough to be washed off with a spray of water. Uncoated film may also be soaked in warm water until it is soft enough to be removed by scrubbing carefully with a brush and water. Steam applied over the film will also remove it. If enzyme-type solutions are used to dissolve the film, it is suggested that the processor wash off the fabric thoroughly with water and then with vinegar to kill the action of the reclaiming agent, so that the solution will not prevent the future adherance of films to the fabric. The screen may be rinsed with water and dried for future use.

In addition to the type of screen washers or reclaimers illustrated in Figure 52, screen-printing shops may also use emulsion and film- remover units which reclaim all fabrics by removing direct emulsions, photographic films, water-soluble films and blockout solutions. These portable removers have a hose attached to the unit which uses a high-pressure spray of warm tap water to blast off the coatings from the screens.

In summary, the textile printer has his choice of various films designed for every type of screen printing. The manufacturer of the film will usually recommend the most practical methods of using and reclaiming or decoating the screens, when the latter is possible.

Chapter X

DIRECT-INDIRECT OR DIRECT-FILM SCREEN

The direct-indirect or direct-film screen differs from the direct screen, although, direct-indirect printing screens also are processed directly on the screen fabric. Essentially, the direct screen is the result of coating a sensitized emulsion on the screen fabric. The direct-indirect screen generally consists of two components: (1) a dry unsensitized film, semi-permanently adhered to a thin plastic backing sheet or to a paper support; and (2) a liquid sensitizer or liquid- sensitized emulsion. However, if the product consists of a presensitized film on a support, then a non-sensitized liquid for adhering the film should be supplied or recommended by the manufacturer of the film.

The direct-indirect or direct-film product became available in the United States in the 1960s.* This type of screen is simple to produce, and since the film bridges the mesh, produces sharp detail in printing. The film adheres well to all fabrics, either fine or coarse, although fine detail may be obtained without using very high mesh counts. Also, manufacturers maintain that because the thickness of the film is predetermined, the strictest control in exposure is not essential, compared with other types of screens. The film provides a tough screen with detail equivalent to that obtained from an indirect screen. In spite of these claimed advantages, it is suggested that the textile printer test each step in the processing of the screen, and standardize his procedures to ensure that the screen will meet his local shop conditions.

The steps in processing this type of screen consist of (1) the preparation of the sensitized emulsion; (2) sensitizing and adhering the direct-film to the screen fabric; (3) drying the screen; (4) exposing; and (5) washing-out. As is true with any screen preparation, before beginning

*Chroma Glo, Inc., Duluth, Minnesota; (U.S. Patent No. 3,532,052)

the printer should have everything prepared and ready.

Preparation of Sensitized Emulsion

Generally the manufacturer or supplier of the direct-film product will include a sensitized emulsion or recommend a sensitizing liquid to use in sensitizing and adhering the film to the screen fabric. Bichromate or diazo-sensitized emulsions may be used. Sensitized bichromate emulsions should be used on the same day they are mixed. However, if they are stored in the dark at room temperature in an opaque container, they may be kept up to one week and used within that time. They may be kept longer, if stored in a refrigerator. Diazo-sensitized emulsions may be kept about three months, if stored in the dark at normal room temperature.

Sensitizing and Adhering Film to Screen

The film may be sensitized and adhered to the screen fabric in one operation. Before starting, a piece of the film is cut so that it is large enough to overlap the design area being printed. The film is placed, emulsion side up, on a perfectly flat built-up surface such as glass, plastic or cardboard (about 1/4" or .64cm thick), as shown in Figure 58A. The screen is centered over the film, with the underside of the screen in direct and complete contact with the emulsion side of the film. The screen fabric which may be clean nylon, polyester, metal cloth or silk should be tightly stretched.

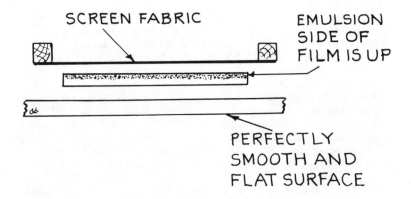

SCREEN FABRIC

EMULSION SIDE OF FILM IS UP

PERFECTLY SMOOTH AND FLAT SURFACE

Figure 58A. **An arrangement of parts for sensitizing and adhering direct-indirect or direct-film to screen fabrics.**

98

Then a little of the emulsion is poured in, on the inside of the screen at one edge, and squeegeed in one or two slow strokes with a round-edged soft squeegee. Make sure that the emulsion has penetrated through the mesh and into the film. The above steps can be done under ordinary incandescent light, but after the sensitized emulsion has been squeegeed into the mesh, the screen should dry completely in the dark. The screen may dry naturally or be force-dried with a fan and warm air that doesn't exceed 86 degrees Fahrenheit (30 degrees Celsius). Diazo-sensitized screens should dry slowly. After the film has dried, the backing sheet or support base can be removed and the screen exposed.

Another method of adhering unsensitized film to the screen fabric before applying the sensitized emulsion is a water-adhering method. In this method the screen is washed until it is completely wet, and the screen is placed on the film. One or two strokes are made with a squeegee on the inside of the screen to ensure that no puddles of water are left in it. The emulsion may then be squeegeed on in the normal manner. The writer has used the water method to stockpile screens for future use by adhering the film to the screen fabric with water only. However, after the film dries and is adhered, the backing sheet must *not* be removed from the film. When it is necessary to prepare a screen, the printer squeegees the sensitized emulsion on the inside of the screen. After the screen dries and before it is exposed, the base or backing sheet is removed.

Exposing

The screen is exposed so that the direct-film is in direct contact with the emulsion side of the positive. Because there is no transparent support or base between the positive and the film, there is a tendency to obtain more perfect reproduction of detail. The exposure will depend on the type of light used, the strength of the light and the distance of the film from the light source. The same types of actinic light sources that are used for exposing direct screens may be used for exposing this type of screen. If the exposure time and the distance of the screen from the light source is not given, the printer may use test strips of opaque tape in a similar fashion to that employed for standardizing the exposure of direct screens.

Washing-Out

The screen may be placed in a vertical position and gently wetted on both sides with cold water. Then a stronger water spray may be directed at the underside or contact side of the screen. Diazo- sensitized screens that have been stored may take a little longer to wash-out. When the image is washed-out and the design appears sharp and clean, the excess water may be blotted with newsprint paper. The screen may be dried naturally or force-dried. Excess emulsion can be used to touch-up or fill-in any open areas.

Reclaiming Screen

After printing and after thoroughly removing the ink with the correct solvent, the direct-indirect screen may be reclaimed in a similar manner to the direct screen. Polyester, nylon and stainless steel screens can be reclaimed with household bleach. One of the ways is to soak the screen in hot water to which bleach has been added. Another way is to soak the screen in hot water and spray or brush the bleach solution on both sides of the fabric. The bleach should remain on the fabric for about five minutes. The screen may then be rinsed off completely with warm water using a hose or a water pressure washer. Generally it is best to use fabrics other than silk, if the fabric is to be reclaimed.

Capillary Direct Film Screen

Since 1965 constant improvement and simplification have occurred with the introduction of new products. An example of such a product is the *capillary direct film* which became available from several manufacturers in 1979. This is a presensitized thick-emulsioned film on a thin transparent polyester support. The film is adhered to the fabric with water prior to exposure. No solvents or chemicals are needed for processing the film. The product consists of a ready buildup of stencil material and does not require any coating of emulsion by the printer. The unexposed presensitized film has a shelf life of six to twelve months, if stored in the dark. After the film is adhered to the screen fabric, it may be stored under dark conditions for about three weeks.

The film may be adhered to monofilament and multifilament mesh, fine or coarse mesh, and is able to print very fine detail and large- area printing, printing thousands of impressions with a screen that has been correctly processed. The capillary quality of the product adheres the film to the print-side of the fabric.

This screen is easy to produce. As is necessary with the preparation of any screen fabric, the fabric must be cleaned or degreased thoroughly before mounting the film on the underside of the screen fabric. It is best to mount the film under a yellow or subdued light. Before mounting, the film should be placed, film side up, on a buildup layer, to ensure complete contact between the film and the fabric. Then the inside of the screen is sponged with water. After one is sure that the film is adhered to the fabric, a firm pass is made with a squeegee to ensure perfect adherance.

The screen is then allowed to dry for about fifteen minutes using warm air that is about 100 degrees Fahrenheit (38C), or until the support sheet is easily removed. The film may then be exposed in contact with a

100

positive to a carbon arc lamp, metal halide lamp, pulsed xenon lamp or to high actinic fluorescent tubes. The rest of the processing is similar to that of the other direct films.

If processed carefully, capillary direct films have proven to be practical for printing on textile materials and for circuit printing.

Figure 59 presents a print made with a capillary film adhered to No. 230 monofilament nylon which was exposed to a pulsed xenon lamp for one minute at four feet (1.22m) from the screen.

Figure 59. A print made with a screen prepared on No. 230 monofilament nylon; the screen was exposed for 60 seconds, at a distance of four feet, to a 5000-watt pulsed xenon lamp. A handmade intaglio positive (plastic drypoint) was used for the original artwork, the fine lines being scratched in on a 1/32″ thick transparent acrylic plastic sheet. In exposing, the positive is placed so that the scratched lines, which are filled-in with ink, are in complete contact with the film on the printing screen.

Chapter XI

TRANSFER PRINTING

Although the beginnings of the art of decorating fabrics are lost in antiquity, dyeing clothing material with strong paper stencils was introduced from China into Japan in the Japanese Nara Era (about 701 to 799 A.D.).* The parts of the stencil were held together with pieces of hair, and later with a silk material. The color was applied by brushing and dabbing.

It was not until the first decade of the 1900s that the principle of screen printing, as we know it today, was developed in the United States. From about 1920 to 1940, some screen-printing problems were being solved, and lacquers, denim-type inks and opaque inks were printed directly on textile materials. Since the 1940s the growth of screen- printing on textiles has greatly accelerated. Today screen printing is not only done directly on bolt material, cut fabrics (before sewing) and finished garments; it is also done by printing varied colored designs on transfer release paper, and then transferring the design from the paper to the textile material with heat and pressure. While the concept of *sublimation* transfer printing dates back to the late 1920s (British patent 922,022 and 349,683), it was not until 1956 that the commercial development of "heat-transfer printing" began. Since its introduction, transfer printing has proved revolutionary for decorating textiles.

Screen printing is a practical method of printing sublimation transfers and of printing plastisol inks on transfer papers. It is able to produce detail and true dye color, multicolor work and halftones on release papers, as illustrated in Figure 60. It is able to print heavier dye deposits, and because of its world-wide use in textile printing, the industry has

*Yoshitaka Kumazawa. *Screen Process Printing in Japan*, Graphic Arts Japan, Vol. 12, 1970-71, pp. 55-57, Japan Printers Assn.

Figure 60. A detailed multicolor design screen-printed on transfer paper for application with the aid of heat and pressure to a textile material. (Courtesy of Photo-Lith International, Scranton, California)

developed materials, techniques and equipment especially for this type of work. Thus, more and more textile printers are not only doing transfer printing manually and semi-automatically, but are installing screen-printing machines for automatic printing. Transfer printing presents the printer with more varied design production and reduces production stoppages for design checks. After it is transferred, the dye is completely fixed, eliminating such processing steps as steaming and washing-off. The process reduces waste compared to printing colored designs directly on garments; also, printed transfers can be die-cut for later transferring. Transfers may be printed manually, may be printed in the general screen-printing shop and of course, in the textile screen-printing shop that is equipped with automatic screen-printing machines and transfer-application machines, as illustrated in Figures 61 through 64A.

Generally, there are two types of screen-printed transfers: (1) those printed with sublimation dyes or inks on transfer release paper; and (2) those printed with plastisol inks on transfer paper. Sublimation dyes are printed only on release papers designed for subsequent transfer to fabric, while plastisol inks may be used for printing directly on fabrics and also on transfer release paper. Chapter XII deals with the subject of plastisol inks and plastisol transfers.

Figure 61. A manual heat-transfer machine used for transferring sublimated and plastisol transfers onto fabric, with adjustable controls, with an on and off switch and a visual pilot light indicator. The timer and thermostat can be set for most types of fabrics. (Courtesy of Naz-Dar Company, Chicago, IL)

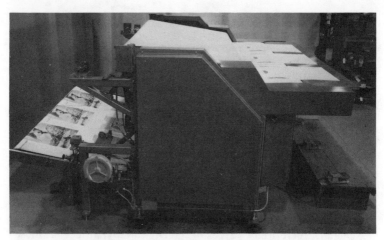

Figure 62. A high-speed heat-transfer machine, with a maximum width of 75" (190.5cm) transfer, allowing three operators to transfer 24" x 30" (61cm x 76cm) designs with a production range of 80 to 120 dozen prints per hour. The machine provides an in-line production of cut parts plus unlimited printing areas with no limitation on the length of the material. The machine can be converted to continuous yard goods transfer printing. (Courtesy of Precision Screen Machines, Inc., Hawthorne, NJ)

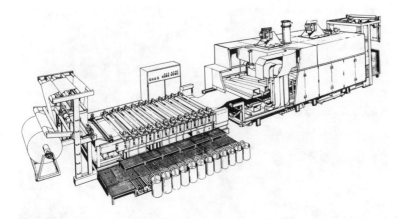

Figure 63. An outline illustration of an automatic rotary screen- printing machine that is available for printing eight to twenty colors in printing widths of 64″ to 126″ (1.63m to 3.20m), with repeat pattern sizes of 25″ to 72″ (63.5cm to 182.9cm) and a machine speed up to 87.5 yards (80 meters) per minute. This machine may be designed to print directly on screen fabrics and also to transfer-print. The machine uses rotary screens for reproducing detail prints. (Courtesy of Stork Brabant, Boxmeer, Holland)

Figure 64. A Dalco Heat Seal Cap Machine designed exclusively for the heat application of transfers to caps. The machine allows wrinkles to be stretched out of the cap's crown before applying the transfer. (Courtesy of Dalco Athletic Lettering Co., Inc., Dallas, TX)

Figure 64A. A table-top cap dryer for producing puff effects with puff plastisol inks on printed caps at about 25 to 30 dozen per hour. Plastisol and puff inks are cured in a single pass through the dryer. (Courtesy of Richardson Industries Corp., Columbus, Ohio)

Chapter XII

PLASTISOL SCREEN PRINTING

The screen-printing industry has produced almost every type of ink, including plastisol, for printing directly on fabrics and for printing on transfer papers. Plastisol inks are thermoplastic inks, and were first used in 1959.

The inks may be applied automatically, semi-automatically and with basic hand-printing units that the beginning printer can purchase or make. The printing of plastisols has motivated the production of equipment specifically for this specialized phase of textile printing and decorating. Because of its advantages in printing, plastisols have aided in the development of all types of garment-printing such as on T-shirts, athletic equipment and cotton blends.

Generally two types of printing are employed—one uses plastisol ink for printing directly on the fabric, and in the other, plastisol is used to print on transfer paper for later transferring to a substrate. The transfer paper used is similar to that employed for sublimation printing. To make the prints more permanent they are cured and polymerized with the application of heat.

Basically, a plastisol ink consists of a polyvinyl resin dispersed or suspended in a liquid plasticizer with other ingredients such as pigments, fillers, modifiers and stabilizers, depending on the desired formulation. Thus, plastisols are the result of a technique which does not dissolve the resin, but disperses it.

Plastisols are also known as dispersion coatings, stretch inks, or organosols formulated for printing on such materials as nylon, open mesh-type fabrics, polyester-cotton blends, polyester acetate, polyvinyl chloride, on release transfer paper, boards, and for printing braille. An organosol is a plastisol containing a volatile dilutent.

107

Printing screens used must be water-soluble ones, photographic lacquer-proof films or paper stencils.

Plastisols are available in a selection of opaque, transparent, translucent, metallic, glitter ink, puff, fluorescent and phosphorescent types. They are also used successfully as adhesives for flocking.

Although the principle of the dispersion technique was developed in 1944*, plastisol inks for screen printing came in the early 1960s. Because these inks have the following advantages, their use has continued to increase. They do not dry in the printing screen and can thus be left in the screen for an unspecified length of time, providing the material is not subjected to heat greater than about 100 degrees Fahrenheit (38C). However, while it is not necessary to air-dry plastisol inks, it is best not to let them set for more than one-half hour before curing or exposing the prints to heat. Plastisols are almost 100 percent solvent-free and do not produce vapors; they cannot be air-dried, because drying implies the evaporation of solvents. The inks may be printed wet-on-wet before heating or curing.

If printed and processed correctly, plastisol inks are practical for printing bright colors directly on dark backgrounds, on knit and woven cotton fabrics, on denim, banners and felt, jackets, all types of T-shirts, on cotton athletic wear, cotton blends, on some synthetics, and generally for printing where high opaque build-up and flexibility are important. The ink bridges loose weaves, forming a three-dimensional, tough, stretchable film after curing. It will withstand being washed in soap and detergent, but may not withstand dry cleaning. Because they retain their color brilliance, plastisols are an important part of colored fabric. Plastisol inks are easy to use. While the ink can be fused on and into most fabric material, it has poor adhesion to nonporous surfaces and some synthetics.

The dry ingredients in the plastisol ink are in suspension, and when the ink is subjected to heat, the resin particles soften, swell and absorb the liquid part, melting together and forming a film on the fabric. In general, homogeneous film-forming will occur when the printed ink reaches a temperature of 250 to 350 degrees Fahrenheit (121 to 177C).

Plastisol inks are available from screen-printing manufacturers and suppliers in many standard and fluorescent colors with instructions for their correct use. There are also inks which print raised or relief effects, simulating embroidery or stitching. If processed correctly, the adhesion of flock to the inks is excellent after curing and even after frequent washing. Flock can be applied to the wet plastisol print electrostatically, manually or with flock guns.

*Glaser, N.A. and Weaver, G.L., "Dispersion Coatings," *Modern Lithography*, Vol. 33, No. 2, pages 71, 73-74, 83, Feb., 1965.

These inks are "cured" rather than dried, since drying implies the presence of volatile solvents. The inks do not air-dry, and curing is accomplished by applying heat to the ink at specific temperatures and for specific lengths of time. Because only curing **solidifies** the ink, it may remain in the screen almost indefinitely without drying. As mentioned earlier, after the ink has been subjected to heat, it forms a continuous elastic rubber-like film with excellent washability. However, because these inks are thermoplastic materials and will melt with the application of heat, dry cleaning is not recommended. Also, it may be practical to wash the printed garment in lukewarm water (about 105 degrees Fahrenheit (41C)). Each ink has its optimum cure temperature and time-length, and using the correct cure determines the durability of the printed image.

For most screen inks, curing is obtained by the evaporation of solids, thermal cross-linkings and UV polymerization in which monomers combine to form a larger crosslinked network of polymers which convert the liquid ink to a solid.

Although the plastisol-printed design may be ironed onto a garment, the heat from the hand-pressing iron must be carefully controlled, as it can cause the design to remelt. There are various heat-curing and drying units (manual or automatic) available that the beginner may use for the application of plastisol and transfer designs to garments and cut pieces (see Figures 61, 62 and 64).

Plastisol designs can be printed wet-on-wet without heat-curing after each printing. After all the colors have been applied, the printed colors may then require a single cure. Ordinarily, the plastisol ink is used directly from the container, after it has been stirred. If any additive is needed, it will be recommended by the manufacturer of the ink.

As mentioned earlier, plastisols may be printed directly on fabric and also on transfer release paper. They may be printed on dimensionally stable, treated paper that has been specifically designed to release the ink pattern. They may be partially fused to the paper, using a lower heat-curing temperature and time-length than for the final curing of the design on the garment. The prints on the paper may be transferred later to a garment or to cut pieces, using the correct heat and pressure for the final curing. Unlike sublimation dye-printed transfers, plastisol inks, in addition to being printed directly on textile materials, will also transfer onto cotton and other materials to which sublimation dye-printed paper may not transfer.

The screen printer may use two types of plastisol transfers: (1) a simple screen-printed transfer; or (2) a screen-printed design with a plastisol white ink coating over the back of the design or image. The white plastisol coating is what adheres to the garment and at the same time

109

carries the design. The backing coating should not be too thick (about three mils) so that transfer may release properly. The image under the white coating can also be applied by means of lithography.

The curing of plastisol prints depends on whether it is done partially on transfer paper, or whether the ink has been printed directly on a garment and then cured. Partial curing is done on transfer prints so that the transfer sheet can be handled and shipped safely. Depending on the ink, partial curing may last from fifteen seconds to about three minutes at temperatures varying from about 225 to 250 degrees Fahrenheit (107 to 121C). The final curing of prints applied directly on fabrics, or transfers applied to garments may vary from about 250 to 360 degrees Fahrenheit (121 to 182C), depending on the ink, the heat applied and the material being decorated with the plastisol. Although infrared radiant energy is often recommended, any heat source that can be controlled may be used to "finalize" the cure. Higher temperatures can be used for a shorter curing period.

Depending on the artwork, coarse multifilament polyester meshes about 4XX to 12XX (about 64 to 125 mesh) or equivalent monofilament polyester fabric, will usually be used for screen-printing plastisols. About 125 to 160 monofilament nylon mesh screens may also be used to print on transfer paper. A rounded, dull squeegee is used for manual printing, applying two or more strokes. The printing screen can be used for printing directly on the fabric or for printing on transfer paper for subsequent release onto fabric. If a garment is placed on a hard surface for direct printing, a softer squeegee, about 50 durometer, should be used. For a single direct printing, a medium squeegee (about 60 to 65 durometer) may be used. For automatic printing, about 8XX or 10XX (79 or about 110 mesh) multifilament fabric may be used for the printing screen.

While all types of printing screens that won't be dissolved by the ink may be employed when printing plastisols, direct-emulsion screens, direct-indirect, lacquer-proof, water-soluble or hand-prepared screens should be used for long runs. Finer detail printing, even four-color process printing, can be printed with 10XX or 12XX multifilament or with 200 monofilament screens.

When printing transfers or iron-on decals on transfer papers, the colors should be printed in reverse order; the last color printed will be the top or uppermost color after the design is transferred to the fabric. Generally, color prints on transfer paper are printed with a sharp durometer squeegee. For multicolor transfer printing, each color is partially fused before the next one is printed, because a fully-fused transfer will not release successfully.

As with sublimation transfers, plastisol-finished transfers are applied in a heat-transfer machine, exercising care when applying the design to

110

heat-sensitive fabrics. In the transfer of designs, the correct temperature, time and pressure are important, and depend on whether a transfer-press, machine or household iron is used. When transferring the design onto the fabric or garment, the transfer is placed ink side down on the material. Heat and pressure are applied for about ten to 30 seconds, the temperature being controlled according to the machine manufacturer's directions, the specifications of the ink manufacturer, and the type of fabric being decorated. If the beginner is working with a print that is small enough for a pressing iron to completely cover the design, a successful transfer may be accomplished with that. Regardless of the heat-source, this step must be pretested and standardized to determine the correct procedure for a successful transfer of the design and appearance of the colors.

Release paper must be cooled (for at least one minute) before releasing the transfer from the substrate. The transfers may be applied to woven or knitted materials, cotton, polyester, nylon and other fabrics recommended by the specific ink's manufacturer. Although the specialist screen printer may use sophisticated heat-curing equipment recommended for curing plastisols, it must be stressed again that the screen printer, regardless of the type of equipment he uses, should make it a practice to pretest each step in the procedure, including washing or dry cleaning and heat-curing the item under his local shop conditions. This should especially be a practice when transferring screen-printed plastisol designs onto unknown or untried fabrics.

Figure 65 presents a multicolor design printed with puff inks on a black acrylic sport shirt. It is suggested that the beginning printer use a simple but attractive one-color pattern for his first printing and transfer. Figure 65A illustrates a multicolor design printed through a monofilament polyester mesh with a plastisol ink for later transferring to a substrate.

Glitter and Puff Inks

Plastisol glitter ink is available for use by the screen printer to produce designs with a visual glitter impact. Glitter plastisol inks contain highly reflective jewel-like particles which are cut into varied small shapes and sizes from brightly-colored aluminum foil or mylar. The plastic mylar is used more often, and is available in many colors. Since this ink consists of highly reflective particles, it provides reflective effects and highlights in the printed design. Because glitter is opaque, the ink will not show through where the glitter has been applied, although glitter is available in silver, gold and colors. Correctly printed and cured glitter ink resists hand or machine washing, but it can't be dry-cleaned.

Glitter ink can be screen-printed directly on the garment or it may be printed on transfer paper for later transferring to fabrics. A coarse monofilament mesh of about 25T to 35T may be used for direct printing, using one or two print strokes. Glitter transfers produce more brilliancy than do images printed directly on textiles. When printing directly on a garment, plastisol inks must be applied first with the glitter ink applied after all the plastisol colors have been printed; it is not practical to place a screen over the glitter. Only one application of glitter is usually applied to prevent diminishing of the glitter effect. Here again, because each fabric will have different characteristics, experimentation is necessary before doing the job.

When printing glitter or jewel-like washable ink, a 15T to 25T screen fabric may be used to produce a heavy deposit. Usually a direct- printing screen is used. Although these inks have been formulated for printing on textile materials and transfer paper, the type of stable release paper used will determine whether the surface will be glossy, matte or dull. A practical paper for glitter is one that has gloss and is transparent. A gloss paper on which transfers may be printed gives the effect of embedded jewels. Direct printing may not produce as brilliant a product as glitter transfers.

After printing, the right combination of time and temperature during curing will provide a correctly finished ink. About three minutes at 300 degrees Fahrenheit (149 C) is common, although whatever is recommended by the manufacturer of the ink should be used. For curing transfer paper, about 1 1/2 minutes at about 250 degrees Fahrenheit (121 C) is often used. After being printed on transfer paper, glitter prints are given a semi-cure, not a full cure; a full cure may be given when the transfer is applied to the fabric.

Figure 65. A multicolor design printed with puff inks on a black acrylic sport shirt.

112

Figure 65A. A multicolor transfer, printed with specially developed products and techniques; the multicolor design was printed with plastisol inks which were heat-applied for fifteen seconds at about 350 degrees Fahrenheit. The carrier sheet was tripped immediately. (Courtesy of Advance-Excello, Chicago, IL)

Figure 65B. A six color screen printed 75-line halftone printed on a T-shirt with plastisol colors through a 350 mesh yellow monofilament polyester screen. (Courtesy of Advance Process Supply Co., Chicago, IL).

113

Puff Inks

Another special ink for printing on textiles is puff ink. This ink was formulated for screen-printing directly on fabrics such as T-shirts to produce an embossed three-dimensional embroidered or stitched effect. Puff inks produce a strong visual impact, are available in desirable colors and are abrasion resistant. In printing, heavy ink deposits may be obtained by using thick stencils and multiple squeegee strokes. The puff or foam effect is produced by exposing the printed design to a special temperature for a specific length of time. Puff inks may be purchased ready-to-use; puff additives for water-base and plastisol inks are also available from ink manufacturers. Although certain plastisols can be mixed with other manufacturer's products, this practice must be recommended by the manufacturer. When printed correctly on such items as T-shirts, hats and flags, puff inks have a wide range of adhesion, stretch and durability. Correctly printed puff designs can be printed on such items in the place of expensive embossed embroidery.

There are two types of puff inks—plastisol and water-base. Both types are opaque, but plastisol puff inks are somewhat more durable. Neither type is intended for printing on textiles which will have to be cleaned. It is not necessary to dry plastisol inks before curing. Water-base puff inks require the use of water-resistant printing screens such as photographic screens or knife-cut lacquer films, screen-printing through about 33T to 100 monofilament screen fabrics.

Plastisol puff inks can be combined with other plastisol inks and may be printed wet-on-wet. When printing multicolor puff inks, it is necessary to cure each color before printing the next. It must be stressed that proper drying and curing are essential for good results. While the curing temperature for water-base may vary somewhat, about 325 degrees Fahrenheit (163 C) for about 1 1/2 minutes is common. Follow the recommendations of the ink manufacturer.

Because an important property of plastisol inks is that they do not dry in the screen, they must be cured to become resistant. This means subjecting the prints to a given temperature for a short period of time in equipment manufactured for that purpose (see Figure 65A). Subjecting the ink to heat produces a swelling of the resin particles, and in the swelling stage the ink absorbs the liquids. As the resin swells, the molecules merge with each other to form a continuous film known as an elastometer (producing polymerization). Manufacturers suggest that the ink should be cured right after the garment is printed and not be allowed to lay around too long.

In summary, since about 1950 the development of textile screen printing has produced specialized inks and equipment that the screen printer is using to apply designs with strong visual impact on a variety of fabrics.

114

Such inks as plastisols, puff and glitter inks may be printed with available equipment in the average screen-printing shop. Although the latter inks are not difficult to print, they are formulated chemicals and should be used as directed by the manufacturer. Also, it is always good practice to pre-test each step.

Figure 65C presents a Braille design printed with puff inks.

Figure 65C. Braille designs printed with puff inks.

Chapter XIII

SUBLIMATION TRANSFERS

Although the first textile-printing job was produced in the United States in 1903, textile printing was confined to printing directly on fabrics until the 1930s. It is amazing to observe the progress textile screen printing has made since then in materials, techniques, patterns for distinctive styling, printing on web or bolt material, on cut fabric pieces, on athletic sportswear and with a textile screen-printing process know as "sublimation printing." Sublimation or heat-transfer printing is really an *indirect* textile-printing process. This transfer process is also known as vapor phase printing, thermoprinting and sublistatic printing—after the Swiss firm Sublistatic SA, which pioneered it. While embroidery transfer prints on textiles have been produced for many years on cotton and linen materials by applying the transfer with a hot iron, modern sublimation heat-transfer printing is a more versatile process.

Essentially, in sublimation heat-transfer printing, a pattern in the form of a dye or ink is screen-printed onto transfer paper. The printed pattern is then transferred from the paper to the fabric with heat-transfer presses (illustrated in Figures 61 and 62), pressing the print from the paper directly against the fabric. Generally, the process requires (1) a special dye or ink for printing; (2) a transfer release paper on which the original printing is done; (3) a transfer unit for transferring the design from the paper to the fabric; and (4) the correct type of fabric onto which the printed patterns may be transferred. In addition to screen-printing the patterns on transfer paper, the process may be accomplished with rotogravure, flexography, lithography and a combination of lithography and screen printing.

The transfer may be accomplished manually, semi-automatically, or automatically on machines built specifically for the purpose. Heat of the exact temperature, the length of the transfer or dwell time, and the

116

pressure between the platen of the heat-unit and the bottom pad are the three most important factors governing correct transfer. The heat-units may have automatically controlled temperature, pressure and exact length of time cycles. During the heat-pressure cycle, the dyes or inks sublime or vaporize, transfer directly to the fabric and are bonded permanently to it. The heat-sensitive dyes color the fabric quickly. After being correctly transferred, the colors are usually fast. For example, for about 90 percent dye development at 30 seconds dwell time, the temperature of the transfer-printing machine calendar may vary from about 374 to 482 degrees Fahrenheit (190 to 220C), depending on the dye color being used.

The dye is printed in reverse on the transfer paper. When transferred to the textile material, the design will appear right-side up. Close and complete contact and pressure between the paper and the fabric should be maintained while the dye is being dispersed and transferred. After the transfer stage, the fabric is dry and usually does not require any after-finishing such as steaming, finishing or drying. This type of screen printing is practical for short runs.

Once the process is set up and standardized, it is accurate, fast and economical, and may be employed for short and long runs. Because finer detail is easier to achieve when printing on paper than when printing directly on fabric, this process can produce intricate multicolor designs and three- and four-color halftone prints on the paper with an accurate registration of colors (see Figure 60). Almost any design that can be printed on transfer paper can be applied to textiles. The process makes it possible to stock only printed paper, rather than the more costly and perhaps obsolete, design-printed fabric. Once standardized, the transfer process is more economical than direct printing, especially for knitted fabrics which may be more difficult to print directly. Transfers also have a lower dye consumption. Because of the heavier dye deposit obtained by screen printing, screen-printed dyes are more brilliant after being heat-transferred.

The mechanical production speed of transfer paper on flat and rotary screen-printing machines is much faster than printing on knitted fabrics directly. For example, when printing transfers on rotary screen-printing machines, as illustrated in Figure 63, paper production speeds of about 65 to 88 yards per minute are possible. All types of printing screens that will not be dissolved by the ink may be used.

Sublimation printing is being done in the textile industry as a separate service or as a supplement to direct printing in the captive shop. The captive shop may be a large part of a parent plant, which prints the paper and transfers the patterns from the paper onto the cloth. Also, paper printers may sell their transfer patterns to others in the textile industry or to smaller establishments which sell transfers for direct, individualized application on their premises.

The sublimation-transfer process is used for printing such items as lingerie, polyester or knit upholstery fabrics, flocked fabrics, rugs, carpet tiles, T-shirts, dress goods, drapes and furnishings. Much transfer printing is being done with disperse colors for transferring to synthetic fabrics such as polyester, blends of polyester and cotton (which may consist of about 67 percent polyester), nylon, acrylic and acetate. However, transfer prints cannot be transferred to all types of fabrics. Sublimation printing is usually not done on natural fibers, although some manufacturers of dyes and transfer papers have developed and are developing papers for fabrics other than polyester.

The transfers may be applied in a textile plant or mill, in the home, in the school as part of an instructional program, or the printed transfer can be purchased and applied in hobby and T-shirt shops that specialize in transfer application. A simple household iron may be used for experimental work done by the beginner, and if the amount of transferring to be done is minimal. A unit of the type illustrated in Figure 61 will answer the needs of the beginner or advanced screen printer who will not do a volume of transfer printing. In large screen-printing plants, the same machine may be employed for printing on transfer paper and for printing directly on cloth, as illustrated in Figure 63. While flat-bed screen-printing machines are practical and are often used, there is a growing tendency toward the development of rotary screen-printing machines, especially in the larger textile- printing plants where both types of machines have been used. Also, conventional rotary screen-printing machines are being modified to print on paper and also directly on fabrics.

Larger textile mills or screen-printing shops that do a large volume of transferring are purchasing equipment of the type illustrated in Figure 62. The transferring process may also be synchronized with the screen-printing process. However, the printer must realize that the fabrics to which printed patterns will be transferred should be pretested for suitability, especially if any doubt exists about the final quality and proper adherance of the transferred design.

While there are other methods of classifying dyes, they are usually classified either by their chemical structure or by their dyeing properties and procedures. Both analyses are applicable to sublimation dyes employed for heat-transfer printing, although the screen printer will be involved mostly with the correct standardized heat-transfer and printing procedures.

Sublimation dyes are heat-sensitive dyes that sublime or have the ability to change quickly under suitable conditions from a solid state to a vapor or gaseous state. These dyes, which are printed on special transfer or release paper, can dye certain textile fibers when the printed dye image is transferred from the paper to the fiber. Unlike plastisol inks, which may also be heat-transferred, sublimation dyes or inks have the ability, under the controlled temperature, pressure and time conditions applied by a heat-transfer unit, to pass from the solid stage to the gaseous stage without going through the liquid stage. Generally, the dyes go through a transition from solid to vapor, not from vapor to solid. If several colors of dye are printed on paper, they should have a similar rate of transfer in order to produce brilliancy and fastness of the colors.

The application of heat increases the spacing between the molecules of a fabric, and the dyes which are in a vapor state and under pressure pass into the fibers, dyeing the material. In the vapor state, the dyes are readily absorbed by such synthetic fibers as plain or woven polyester and polyester blends. Because of transfer-printing's success, research may yet develop techniques for transfer-printing dyes on natural fibers.

Sublimation inks have been formulated for printing on flat and rotary screen-printing machines and also for manual printing. A sublimation dye, ink or paste consists of microscopically ground dye particles that are in a resin system carrier with solvents and additives. The type of textile to which the printed designs are ultimately transferred and the end use of the product determine the specific properties of the dye used to print on transfer paper. The dyes, like everything else in the total process—inks, paper, machines and processing variables—must be specifically integrated for successful results. The beginner or the advanced textile screen printer may obtain help from the dye or ink manufacturer, the paper manufacturer or distributor or from the supplier of the heat-transfer equipment.

The choice of transfer paper is important, because the paper does influence the quality of the transfer. Transfer-printing requires a high quality special or coated paper to produce successful sublimation and transfer. The paper must serve as an ideal support and carrier for the printed dyes which are ultimately transferred to the fabric. The paper should have good dye release and not be too absorbent, to eliminate dye retention. Transfers or release papers are available from paper merchants, paper mills, screen-printing suppliers and ink and dye manufacturers. While transfer paper requirements may vary somewhat, the following papers have been used successfully as transfer or release papers in the major printing processes: glassine parchment, machine- glazed paper, unglazed paper, bond, single-coated paper, unporous bleached kraft paper that is smooth on one side, coated book paper with a calendered finish and specially coated stock developed for sublimation printing. The paper may be uncoated, double-coated or single-coated. Ordinarily, the printing is done on the coated side. There is no one universal paper that will serve all transfer-printing purposes—there are papers for printing transfers on acrylics, papers for increasing color brightness and papers for printing on carpet tile. Thus, if the screen printer is in doubt about the printing and transfer quality of a paper, he must test it in the various steps of the procedure, including the transferring of patterns.

The basic weights of the types of paper used are 35, 51, 52 and 55 pounds (the weight is the weight of 3,000 square feet of a given paper). While a lighter weight paper may be recommended for manual printing, medium and heavier weight paper are recommended for semi-automatic and automatic printing. Some textile transfer printers suggest that the paper be as thin as possible to reduce its insulating effect between the heat-source and the dye.

Several different types of paper may be used for transfer-printing. Generally, porous paper is not recommended, because it can absorb the dye and prevent it from transferring. Although the ink should adhere, it should not penetrate the paper. Penetration may prevent the dye from transferring perfectly to the fabric. For textile heat-transfer printing, the paper must accept and hold the print for a given time period and then release the dye pattern during the transferring stage.

The paper should be dimensionally stable so that it can be easily printed. It should not be too flexible, and it should not curl or stretch under heat and pressure. The dye should adhere and not come off during the handling and storage of the printed paper.

Most transfer papers are translucent so that the print can be more easily seen and positioned on the fabric. The dye color printed on the paper may differ from the resulting color obtained after transferring. To obtain the correct final color of the transferred dye, the correct dwell time must be used. Again, this implies that the screen printer must test each new color by doing transferring under his own shop conditions.

The general acceptance of the process by major textile printers, by knitting mills and converters; the employment of detailed and versatile scenic photographic work and creative designs; and the availability of materials, equipment and information have forced heat-transfer printing to come of age in a very short period of time. Today, the progressive textile printer and the general screen printer who can accept challenges and develop new processing steps, may find heat-transfer printing to be either a viable supplement to his general screen-printing or a practical printing specialty.

In summary, while the concept of sublimation transfer-printing dates back to the 1920s, it was not until 1956 that commercial heat transferring developed as we know it today. It has solved its initial problems of suitable dyestuffs (inks) and paper substrates, has developed correct equipment for transferring the image onto fabric, and has stressed the use of the correct steps in processing. It has become a process which supplements general textile screen-printing. Heat- transfer printing is being done in the textile industry as a separate service to direct printing in the in-house shop or captive shop. The process is employed for producing such items as lingerie, upholstery fabric, flocked fabrics, rugs, carpet tiles, dress goods and drapes.

Chapter XIV

IMPRINTED SPORTSWEAR AND OTHER GARMENTS

Imprinted sportswear such as T-shirts and denim garments are not new. The process was started in the early 1920s by pioneer screen printers and helped motivate an industry of imprinted garments and fabrics. Most of the screen-printing done by the early printer was done directly on such materials as denim, cotton, sign cloth and automobile tire covers, with oil-vehicle-type opaque inks, lacquers and denim-type inks. As inks and the experience of the printer improved, screen- printed sportswear became more common in the 1930s, and the mass- production of designs on athletic garments became a reality in some of the general screen-printing shops. Although the earlier inks were not of today's dye quality, they did produce a flexible film of considerable thickness and allowed a dark-background fabric to be effectively covered with a variety of opaque colored prints. Due to the weight of the material, "hand" was not much of a factor. Some ingenious early printers even screen-printed one or two colors, and then airbrushed one or more colors on the garment to produce special effects.

Lacquers are still being used for direct-printing on such items as neckties, shopping bags, banners, novelty pillowcases and raincoats. They provide excellent adhesion, and may be washed or dry cleaned. Lacquers and denim-type inks do not require heat-curing or heat-setting to make the ink fast.

Denim inks may also be printed directly on such items as T-shirts, linens and synthetic fabric garments, with minimum penetration. The inks were and are formulated for printing on top of such heavy fabrics as felt and twill denim. These may be opaque, heavy-bodied, flexible long oil-alkyd formulations, and may be printed with medium, rounded, soft-edged squeegees. They have excellent opacity and generally air-dry by oxidation in about three to eight hours. Some manufacturers suggest that they be allowed to dry (age) for about a week. Some experienced T-shirt printers recommend this aging period before the first washing of the printed garment. When printing one color over another, the first color should be allowed to dry one to four hours before the second is applied; or it may dry overnight under normal atmospheric conditions. While air-dry inks do not require heat in order to cure properly, they may be run through a dryer, if one is available and the printer is in a hurry.

Even in the early days, it was evident that screen-printing on T-shirts and athletic wear was a form of immediate mass communication. Originally, imprinted sportswear was considered a fad that was used mostly for souvenir items and for athletic team groups, fraternities or clubs. Today it has grown into a very important part of the screen-printing industry. The development and perfection of photographic screen printing, equipment, inks and dyes has greatly added to the decorating of all types of sportswear and other textile products. However, it was not until the 1970s that printing and decorating T-shirts became a vital phase of screen printing, with small T-shirt shops, large firms and shopping malls offering the imprinting of sportswear. Perhaps the reason for the acceleration of this growth is that printing T-shirts is still a business or hobby that can be started up with little financial investment. It must also be stressed that the development of plastisol inks, sublimation dyes, heat-applied graphic designs, heat-transfers and related equipment and materials have accelerated this growth, especially the imprinting of T-shirts. While imprinting may be done on a variety of garments, T-shirts, sweat shirts and doubleknit shirts have been produced more often than other garments. Usually, the screen printer uses white T-shirts, T-shirts with a white or light contrasting neck and arm trim or full-colored shirts, as illustrated in Figure 66.

An imprinted T-shirt is a medium of instant communication. Considering the length of time that the message can be used, T-shirts provide very inexpensive advertising. This type of printing, used for many types of communication, may express an instant message with great impact and humor. The wearing of a garment with a printed or heat-applied transfer allows the wearer to communicate a message without inhibition; an individual may even have his picture or likeness reproduced on his garment. Not only do imprinted garments display every type of message design for men, women and children—the creative printer has succeeded in making T-shirts an accepted fashion item worldwide, suitable to varied interest groups.

The novice must realize that this type of printing does require a knowledge of art production or the purchase of an art service, experience in screen printing, knowledge of printing-screen processing (if one is to process his own screens), a knowledge of related materials and equipment to produce quality work for the various processing steps, a work area and the storage space for screens and repeat designs. Screens can

123

Figure 66. The P-110 Manual single T-shirt printer with a shaped platen for positioning the garment, with a self-supporting lift for holding the screen up and a mounting for bolting or clamping the printer to a bench. (Courtesy of Ranar Manufacturing Co., Los Angeles, CA)

be stored for future jobs by hanging them in a rack that is suspended from the ceiling. This saves floor space for other activities in the shop. At first, the new owner or hobbyist may be the manager, buyer, artist, printer, salesperson and delivery service all at once. However, if the printer is the owner of a general screen-printing shop, the imprinting of sportswear may serve as a specialty to supplement his other services.

As far as the production of T-shirts and other imprinted sportswear is concerned, the printer should realize that competition has made the buying public more selective in its purchases. The items in many instances are being marketed directly to the consumer, and the use of much color and detail, fabric blends, and design-imprinting on women's T-shirts and fashion tops has aided in producing a constantly growing market.

Heat-Transfer Printing

The printer is employing the following heat-applied imprinting production techniques: hot-melt wax transfers, litho-printed screen-backed transfers, plastisol transfers, rhinestone transfers, sublimation-dye transfers and even electrified transfers. If the printer does not print his

124

own transfers, he may purchase them from varied suppliers for application to garments. Although heat-transfers were produced by gravure printng in the early 1900s, their use grew and was standardized with the development of the correct inks, transfer paper and heat-transfer equipment.

Hot-melt wax transfers were used more often in the 1950s and were applied with a hot iron to the garment. The inks employed for printing these transfers consisted of waxes, resins, pigments and plasticizers, and were formulated to remain solid at room temperature. The transfers may be printed on sheets or in roll form, and can be printed in multicolor designs. The transfer is released hot, and may be applied mechanically to any fabric.

In the litho-printed screen-backed transfer, the design is first lithographed (or screen-printed) on a transfer release paper. Then a white plastisol ink coating of about three or more mils in thickness is printed over the image. The design may be detailed and multicolored or a halftone. The screen-printed backup coating binds the printed design to the fabric during transferring. A glitter effect can be produced by printing a glitter ink or by adding a jewel-type glitter to the plastisol; the plastisol-glitter ink may be used as a backup coating. However, glitter-plastisol inks should be heat-fused as quickly as possible to prevent too much ink from penetrating into the garment. The beginner should make a complete trial transfer after printing, especially to standardize such factors as transfer and dwell time. The plastisol transfer, sublimation-type dye transfer, and the lithographed-backed transfer are the most often used for imprinting sportswear.

A patented electrified heat-transfer with light-emitting diodes embedded in it further extends the versatility of the heat-transfer process. The transfer is pulled apart for installation or application to the garment. Two thin wires leading from the transfer are connected to a battery which can be held in the pocket of the garment's wearer. Generally, the light-emitting diodes will last for the life of the garment. The garments may be hand washed.

The ink used is very important if the best results are to be obtained, whether one is printing directly on garments or onto transfer release paper. Because T-shirts and sportswear are made of natural, synthetic, and synthetic and natural blend fabrics, the choice of an ink is an important step and should be based either on the manufacturer's recommendation or on test printing. The type of artwork, the type of fabric, the thickness of the fabric, drying, heat-curing, the equipment used, the printing screen and the experience of the screen printer are all factors in the choice. Inks are available in a variety of colors, and generally may be screened through a recommended polyester or nylon screen fabric mesh. There are many formulated screen-printing inks available, but the printer usually uses water-phase or water-soluble inks, air-set inks, water-and-oil emulsion inks and of course, plastisol and sublimation inks (see Chapter XII and XIII). Plastisol inks are easy to print and enable the printer to decorate any colored fabric, from white to the darkest shade. Plastisol inks can be printed directly on garments or on transfer release paper; sublimation ink is usually printed on release paper and then transferred to the garment. Most inks are durable when properly used, dried and cured.

Water-soluble, water-based or aqueous inks are thermosetting types of pigmented inks, as shown in Figure 52A. The reader must realize that water-based inks were used prior to the 1970s by sign painters and some screen printers. However, the need for water-based ink became more obvious in 1973 as a possible solution to alleviate the excessive demand for petrochemicals, and as a possible solution to the problem of the world oil shortage. Pigments became available in the 1930s for textile printing, and the availability of the pigments indirectly aided in the development of water-based inks.

Generally, a water-based system is one in which the pigment is dispersed in a water emulsion. An emulsion consists of minute drops of a liquid that are suspended in a second liquid with which the first will not mix. For example, it may be a finely divided suspension of oil in water, or of water in oil. It is interesting to note that water-based inks (water-in-oil emulsions) have been used since the 1940s for textile printing; this was a development of the Inmont Corporation (Interchemical Corp.). Most printing today is done with water-in-oil emulsions. The material printed with this type of ink becomes non-aqueous after it is dried, baked or cured to polymerize the binding medium. Binders, pigments and solvents in the oil-in-water and the water-in-oil type are similar.

According to today's manufacturers, water-based inks offer the following advantages. In addition to needing only water or water and a detergent to wash them from the screen, the inks render high definition in printing, are odor-free, are generally non-toxic and are available in brilliant transparent colors. Two or more transparent colors may be printed to produce more colors on a substrate. There are also opaque water-based inks and metallic colors for printing on dark backgrounds; the colors are lead-free. Water-based inks do not contain flammable solvents; consequently they have been recommended for use in schools. Water-based inks can be used for printing on cotton, polyester, cotton and polyester blends, rayon, linen, fiber glass and other synthetic fibers. They generally dry to a soft "hand" finish, and one color may be printed over another "wet-on-wet" to obtain multicolor prints. Water-based inks will dry in about 40 minutes; the printed goods may be cured in about three minutes at about 325 degrees Fahrenheit (163C), depending on the ink and the dryer. However, if water-based inks are to be printed for the first time on any given fabric, every step of the process should

Figure 67. A "Vastex" manual T-shirt printer designed for printing six colors in accurate registration, holding the fabric taut and allowing for the simultaneous printing of a design area from 10" x 10" (25cm x 25cm) to 19" x 19" (48cm x 48cm). If transparent type dyes are being printed, more colors may result when colors are overprinted. (Courtesy of Naz-Dar Company, Chicago, IL)

be pretested before starting a production run. One of the steps in the processing is to ensure that the water in the ink evaporates before it is cured.

Water-soluble or water-based inks must be printed with a screen that is resistant to water-based inks. While the design will govern the choice of mesh to be used for printing, 200 to 400 monofilament polyester or nylon is often used in the preparation of the printing screen. Because water-based inks are being printed more and more on pressure-sensitive decals, vinyl-coated products, book covers and signs, it is maintained that water-based inks will be used in the future where solvent-based inks are used today.

Air-set inks may be printed wet-on-wet. The inks do not require heat-treatment, although accelerated drying may be employed if desired. They may be totally cured in about seven days under normal atmospheric conditions, depending on the printing instructions and the amount of humidity present in the working area. They are practical for use on cotton and other light-color absorbent fabrics. Some of the inks will dry in about 30 minutes. Air-set inks should be printed on unsized fabrics.

127

Figure 68. A Precision Oval T-Shirt Printer which has a print area from 16 1/2" x 18" (42cm x 46cm) to 24" x 30" (61cm x 76cm), prints on T-shirts, sweatshirts and cut pieces of varied fabrics, decorates four to eight colors in a production capacity from 75 dozen to 150 dozen per hour, depending on the set-up. The unit allows for the printing of two separate designs simultaneously. (Courtesy of Precision Screen Machines, Inc. Hawthorne, NJ)

Water-and-oil emulsion-type inks are employed for printing on all types of sportswear. They also may be screened wet-on-wet and can be heat-cured at about 350 degrees Fahrenheit (177C) for about three minutes. These inks can be cleaned off the printing screen with the manufacturer's recommended solvent. The inks can be printed on cotton T-shirts, linen, burlap, percale and combinations of fabrics.

The need for versatility in decorating T-shirts and sportswear has produced a choice of a variety of equipment and materials for manual, semi-automatic and automatic printing, as illustrated in Figures 66, 67 and 68. General equipment may consist of a printing unit or machine, a process camera or enlarger, a light-exposing source, printing screens, a dryer and a heat-transfer machine. If the printer is handy with tools, he may build a first printing unit to suit his needs. However, it may be more practical to purchase a new or used unit. Any piece of equipment should be purchased only if there is a definite need for it. If the beginner plans to print one color for most of his work, then he should purchase a one-color printer as his first unit (see Figure 66).

If a garment has a tendency to stick to the underside of the screen, making it necessary to peel off the garment, it may be practical to apply a semi-permanent adhesive to the platen or base of the unit. In addition to T-shirts, these units will print on jackets, bowling shirts, emblems, pennants, cut goods, flags and napkins. Some of the single-color printers are designed so that more screens can be added to the unit for printing more colors. The available machines accurately locate the areas on which the design is to be printed, render the fabric instantly taut, locking it firmly in place for printing. Figure 68 illustrates an oval multicolor printer which requires one operator to load and unload the printed matter; the rest of the work is done automatically. Some of the machines are built to have an "XYZ" registration, or to register the garment horizontally and vertically in both directions. The machines are designed to print on all weights of fabric, to print wet-on-wet and to print up to seven colors. They can print more intermediate colors by over-printing one transparent ink on another transparent ink. Manually-operated machines do not require wiring or electrical connections; those that do are designed so that they may be connected to standard electrical outlets. Print areas vary from about 10" x 10" to 20" x 20"; presses with larger print areas can be built to order.

In the manual or semi-automatic carousel printer, the screen is plac-ed in the screen holder of the unit and aligned in correct position with the designs in the screens. When the garment is placed on the platen or base of the first screen, the screen is lowered and the first color is printed by pulling the squeegee slowly across. When the screen is raised, the unit is rotated manually or mechanically to the second position, and the second color is printed. The rest of the colors are printed in a similar fashion.

As his volume of printing increases, the printer may also need a dryer (see Figures 69 and 70) for drying and curing plastisol inks, sublimation-type prints and other textile ink prints. The screen printer may have a dryer that uses forced air (convection) coupled with infrared heat (ra-diant energy). The dryer may have a conveyor belt on which the printed garments are placed to pass under a heat-unit or through a long tunnel. The speed of the conveyor and the curing time are governed by the type of ink printed, the type of fabric printed and the recommended time of curing or drying for the specific garment. Regardless of the type of unit, the dryer should have an adjustable temperature control or an ad-justable means of elevating the heat source above the work, and a variable belt speed. While the width of the tunnel may be built to the printer's specifications, widths usually vary from about 24" to 48". Most dryers have adjustable height for the heat panel (to ensure that the garment is

Figure 69. A Vastex Infrared Dryer designed for drying and curing textiles and for other specialized uses, it is available in lengths up to fourteen feet (4.27m) with a conveyor belt width of up to 48 inches, and (122cm) with variable belt speed and temperature adjustment. (Courtesy of Vastex Co., Inc., Somervill, NJ)

Figure 69A. A Capri Radiant Textile Dryer that handles both caps and T-shirts, is designed to cure plastisol inks, curing all portions evenly. The unit has a radiant output of 1800 watts, an insulated curing chamber, temperature control and a variable speed conveyor. (Courtesy of The Advance Group, Chicago, IL)

130

not scorched) and a variable conveyor speed to match production rates and curing time. Dryers are also available with modules or parts that may be added if the production requires a longer dryer. Figure 69A presents a radiant textile dryer for drying and curing caps and T-shirts printed with plastisol inks.

Any type of resistant printing screen that will not be dissolved by the printed ink may be used, although direct screens, direct-indirect or direct-films and knife-cut printing screens are used most often for printing T-shirts and similar sportswear. Generally, when printing plastisols, 6XX to 10XX screen fabric or equivalent monofilament polyester or nylon are used in the preparation of the screen. For printing detailed sublimation ink designs, finer monofilament mesh (up to 305) may be used. If the printing screens are made in the local shop, the operator must develop the habit of precision processing.

Heat Transfer Machines

Since heat-applied graphics are based on the application of heat to a design being transferred on a garment, heat transfer equipment is a very important part of the interdependent process of decorating T-Shirts and other garments. The printer will use these machines to apply plastisol and sublimation type ink designs on T-shirts, caps, emblems on sleeves and other fabric items. If the novice or hobbyist does not have a heat transfer machine available, the transfer may be made with a household iron. However, the heat and pressure will not be as easily maintained as with a commercial machine.

Most heat transfer machines are basically similar in their application of the design transfer, whether it is applied manually, semi-automatically or automatically. Manually operated units, as shown in Figure 61, are practical for the first machine, for experimental work where its use may be infrequent or even for store applications. A semi-automated unit is suggested if adjustable heat, pressure and dwell time, and greater volume are required. A fully automatic machine, as illustrated in Figures 62 and 63, which is completely adjustable in all respects, may be used for heavy duty every-day production. In addition to the availability of standard heat transfer unit machines, there are also manual and automatic units available for transferring designs and letters onto such items as caps, tennis shoes, cuffs, shoe strings and sleeves.

The procedure for applying a heat transfer to a garment is fairly simple. The garment is placed on the lower platen in the heat transfer machine. The transfer is placed, ink side down, in contact with the garment. The machine is set at the correct temperature (which may be about 325 to 375 degrees Fahrenheit (163 to 190 C)), and pressure is applied for about fifteen seconds. However, the correct temperature and time should be determined by experimentation or by the manufacturer's recommendation. Release paper should not be removed from the garment until the paper has cooled. Each garment should be properly cured to prevent the design from fading. A heavier garment may require more heat or a longer dwell time. Of course, it is important that the heat unit always deliver the right amount of heat. If a machine is used constantly, there should be no fans or strong drafts blowing on it, as excessive air movement may lower the heat temperature.

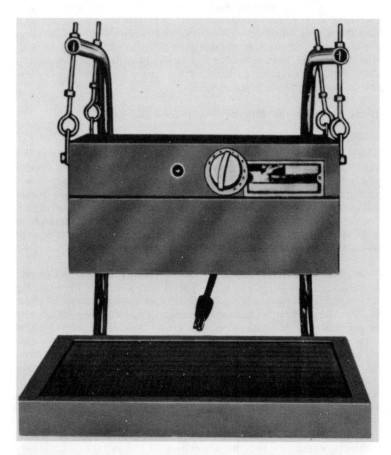

Figure 70. A Lawson Infrared Drying Unit designed for drying and curing plastisol and water-based inks on T-shirts, nylon jackets and heat transfers on paper, equipped with a proportionate heat controller and adjustable height of the heat panel to the work. The unit may also be used to test-cure different types of inks and to test samples of printed garments. (Courtesy of Lawson Printing Machine Co., St. Louis, MO)

The pressure exerted should be enough to apply the transfer to the garment. The printer must experiment at first to find the amount of manual or machine pressure that is practical. For example, in applying glitter transfers that have a heavy build-up, some printers will insert an old transfer paper on the inside of the garment before placing it down on the platen or press, and then apply pressure. The paper inside the garment may prevent the heavy glitter transfer from going through the garment and adhering the back and front of the shirt.

The availability of materials, equipment, production techniques and information for imprinting on sportswear and other garments stresses the fact that the potential of this phase of screen printing or mitography is unlimited.

Figure 71 illustrates two multicolored T-shirts; each shirt was screen printed with a design technique explained in this chapter. One of the shirts ("Octoberfest" design) was printed with a plastisol ink, and the other shirt was printed with a water-based screen printing ink.

In summary, the screen printer, the screen printing industry and the textile printing industry will continue to develop new methods and

Figure 71 presents an illustration of two screen printed T-shirts made up of 50 percent polyester and 50 percent cotton. The multicolor "Shriner" design was printed directly on a white shirt with a water-based textile; the "Octoberfest" design was printed directly on a light blue shirt with a dark brown and white plastisol ink. (Courtesy of Penncraft, Inc., Rosemont, IL)

133

equipment for printing on all types of textiles. Because in our industrial society changes are constantly taking place, the textile printer must be cognizant of the important developments that may affect him. Emerging and developmental needs will continue to motivate the growth of screen printing and related industries so that the sum total of these industries may continue to add to the technical, socio-economic and cultural development of society.

Chapter XV

TEXTILE DISCHARGE
SCREEN PRINTING

Although there are other methods of screen-printing on textiles, the printer generally uses three types: (1) **direct printing;** (2) **transfer printing**; and (3) **discharge printing**. In the first type, he applies color to the fabric in a variety of means, the color having the ingredients and properties necessary to be absorbed and fixed onto the textile fiber. In transfer printing (see Chapter XI), the design is first printed on transfer release paper and then transferred to a fabric. In discharge screen printing, the printer produces white or colored effects on a darker background of ground colored textile material. In this type of printing, the cloth is dyed and then the dyed color is removed. This is accomplished with printing pastes that contain chemicals which remove, extract or discharge the ground color, and at the same time print a new and lighter color in the discharged areas.

In discharging, the dye is chemically destroyed on the fibers without damage to the fibers. But, the discharge paste used must not destroy the new color that is to be printed. In discharge printing, the dyeing of the ground dark color is done so that it can be discharged by a chemical known as a reducing agent. In "white discharging," a color is not added to the discharge paste; the ground color is removed and the cloth is left white in the discharge-printed areas. In "color discharge printing," discharge resistant dyes are added to the print paste. These dye pastes replace the original background color in the cloth. It must be noted that discharge printing can only be accomplished if the color can be discharged.

It is not practical to print light-colored small patterns and then print the dark background color around the design or blotch areas (the printed background of a pattern). Therefore, discharge printing is used for the removal of dark color and for producing the original white or pale col-

135

or with another color printed in its place at the same time. For example, the printer may start printing on a cotton material which is dyed blue; he wants to produce white, red and yellow on the cloth. Because dyes are transparent and not opaque, he cannot print the colors directly on the blue, as a combination of the printed color and blue would be the result. Neither can he print white or the original color of the material. (This may be done with opaque-type coatings such as lacquers or enamels but will not produce a dye effect.) Therefore, he will print three discharge pastes, each containing chemicals or ingredients capable of removing the ground color. One of the pastes printed will discharge the color without adding another color in the discharged spots. This is known as white discharging, because a color is not added to the discharge paste. The two other pastes (for discharge printing red and yellow) will each contain one of these colors and the correct proportion of ingredients for printing the color and for making sure that it will be fixed.

The chemicals used for discharging colors are known as reducing agents, alkalis, oxidizing agents, acids, acid salts, alkali salts and china clay (kaolin). The chemical that is usually used as the discharging agent is known as sodium sulfoxylate formaldehyde (sodium sulfoxylate). For colored discharge printing the dyestuff or color included in the discharge paste must withstand the action of the reducing agent. For white discharge printing, sodium sulfoxylate can be dissolved in water (about one part by weight to four parts by weight of water), and this solution is then mixed with an equal solution by weight of a gum tragacanth-starch mixture. The printer should realize that this proportion is more or less a starting point and that every discharge formula will be slightly different depending on the chemical nature of the ground color and the material to be dyed. The manufacturer of the dye will recommend which of his colors discharge best and which fabrics can be discharged. If one does not know whether a color can be discharged on a given material, tests must be performed to determine its suitability for discharge printing. Often the range of colors that may be discharge printed is limited. After discharge printing, both the ground color and the printed discharge pattern must be fast.

Colors used for discharge printing generally use the same color formulation with the discharge paste as is used in regular textile printing. On heavier dyed material the amount of the reducing agent may need to be increased. It is suggested that the printer first try a manufacturer's discharge paste, and that he perform white discharging or just discharging of the ground color before he tries discharge color printing.

The treatment of the cloth after discharge printing is similar to its treatment after regular textile screen printing—the discharge- printed cloth is dried, aged or steamed, rinsed well, soaped (if necessary), rinsed again and dried. Thus, discharge printing does involve knowledge of general textile screen printing, in addition to knowledge of the fabric

136

printed on, of the ground color, of discharge paste formulations, of heat or steam application, and of all the post-printing treatments.

Experimentation with equipment and materials, the correct formulation of discharge pastes and the use of the manufacturer's recommendations are all necessary for successful discharge printing. If the discharging is not done correctly, semi-discharging (partly white) may be the result; over-discharged cloth may become tendered or deteriorated. Vat, basic, direct, mordant, azoic and some pigment colors may be discharged.

Discharge screen printing offers the advantage of producing any type of detail on cloth. Also, it deposits a thick coating of paste for the detail printing. This type of screen printing may be used for sample work, for large-volume work, for personalized work such as the printing of initials on ties and for promotion or point-of-purchase work.

It must be stressed that discharge printing differs from resist printing. In the latter process, a resist paste (resin, paste, wax-type or chemical resist) is printed on the white dyed cloth before the actual printing or dyeing is done. The resist prevents the printed color from penetrating into the areas where the resist was printed. The resist is removed after the dyeing process is completed.

Discharge formulas are rather complex chemical compounds, and it is not practical for the beginning printer to completely prepare his own formulations. However, a variety of formulas for discharging ground dyes from cloth materials are available with which the printer may experiment and mix. When doing commercial discharge printing, the printer should first make trial prints, especially when he plans to do large-volume printing. The following descriptions of formulas are presented, not to encourage the use of certain commercial products, but to show the variations of formulas. The ingredients in each formula are mixed in the order in which they appear. Because pigmented-type dye pastes are often used by the printer, the first formula presented for discharge printing deals with a pigmented emulsion.

I. DISCHARGE PRINTING ON COTTON
WITH AQUAPRINT COLORS

Aquaprint[1] colors are applied on textile materials in the form of pigmented oil-in-water emulsions. They may be screen-printed on cotton, rayon, acetate, polyamide, acrylic, triacetate, polyester, glass and other natural and synthetic and blend fibers. Numbers 10, 12 or coarser screen fabrics may be used, depending on the type of fabric and the pattern to be printed. The printing can be done manually, semi-automatically or automatically. Direct photographic screens, direct-indirect screens,

[1] Inmont Corporation, Hawthorne, NJ

gelatin films or gelatin coatings reinforced with enamels, knife-cut films, and tusche-glue screens which employ enamels or varnish (instead of glue) for the permanent filler may all be used for the preparation of the printing screens.

To do textile discharge screen-printing on cotton and rayon with these pigmented colors, the printer will need (1) a "clear" emulsion carrier, medium or vehicle; (2) other ingredients and colors which are mixed into the clear; (3) some containers in which to do the mixing; and (4) any type of high-speed mixer that is driven by an explosion-proof motor.

Because discharge printing is similar to regular or application- textile printing, the preparation of the cut clear and the mixing of the colors is similar.

Preparing Cut Clear for Discharge Printing

The preparation of the printing emulsion for discharging consists first of (1) making the cut clear; (2) adding the selected colors; (3) adding another clear recommended by the manufacturer for the reduction of crocking and for improving fastness in washing; and (4) adding gum carriers and sodium sulfoxylate formaldehyde.

The first step in the preparation of the printing paste is the mixing of the cut clear. A variety of concentrated clears are available for making what is known as a cut clear to which the color and several other ingredients are added. The following is a typical formula for the preparation of a cut clear that can be used for both discharge printing and application printing:

Components for Cut Clear	Parts by Volume
a. Aquaprint Clear Concentrate 5928	2 gallons
b. Water	50 gallons
c. Solvent (Mineral Spirit such as Varsol[2] No. 2)	48 gallons
	100 gallons

Although the above formula is given in gallons, the printer may want to try mixing smaller proportions for trial printing.

To make the cut clear, measure out the water in a suitable container or drum. Mix the clear concentrate with an equal volume of the solvent or mineral spirit. Then add the clear concentrate and solvent to the water in the container while the mixer is running, allowing the three to mix well. Add the rest of the mineral spirits slowly while the mixer is running, continuing on high-speed mixing for fifteen minutes. The viscosi-

[2] Humble Oil and Refining Co., Houston, TX

ty of the cut clear formula can be varied by changing the amount of the clear concentrate; use a smaller amount to decrease viscosity and a larger amount to increase viscosity

Preparing Emulsion for Discharge Printing

After the cut clear is mixed with the water and the solvent, add to it the selected color which is to be discharge-printed and mix thoroughly with a high-speed mixer. Generally, twice the volume of cut clear is mixed with one volume of color to make a deep shade.

To the clear and color mixture add Aquaprint Auxiliary Clear 5949, using five percent for light-color shades and fifteen percent for dark shades of color. Mix well.

Finally, prepare the following solution in parts by volume:
a. 6% Aqualized gum tragacanth or other suitable
gum carrier...........................25 parts
b. 50% Solution of sodium sulfoxylate
formaldehyde...........................75 parts
and add the desired amount of the latter mixture to the clear-color-auxiliary clear mixture. This is the discharge-printing emulsion. It must be stressed that in making up the discharge-printing emulsion the maximum amount of sodium sulfoxylate formaldehyde that can be included is one pound per gallon, or equivalent amounts depending on the proportions of the formulation. The sodium sulfoxylate formaldehyde must be added in a gum carrier in order to maintain proper printing viscosity and to aid in emulsion stability.

After screen printing to produce the discharge effects, the cloth should be dried, aged or cured for three minutes at 300 degrees Fahrenheit, washed and dried again. In regular or application printing with Aquaprint colors, the cloth is dried to allow volatile materials to be driven off and then heat-cured.

II. FORMULA FOR PRODUCING WHITE DISCHARGE PRINTING ON COTTON

Cottons are usually dyed with dischargeable direct colors. The following is a formula[3] for producing a white discharge:
a. 10% sodium sulfoxylate
b. 30% water (lukewarm). Stir into
c. 50% Polygum[4] 260, or Keltex[5], add
d. 10% titanium dioxide (1:1)

————————
100%

[3] General Aniline and Film Corp., Easton, PA

139

A cotton cloth discharged with the above formulation should be dried, steamed for five to ten minutes in a neutral rapid ager, rinsed well in cold water, soaped at 90-100 degrees Fahrenheit, again rinsed in cold water and dried.

Add vat colors to the above formula for colored discharge printing on cotton. They are applied with the normal vat-color printing procedure that is recommended for regular application printing.

III. FORMULATION FOR DISCHARGE PRINTING ON SILK

Silks are usually dyed with dischargeable acid colors. Color discharge printing on silk is done with selected acid and basic colors which are not affected by sodium sulfoxylate. The following is a formula[3] for discharge color printing on silk:

> a. 2% Color
> b. 2% Glycerin A
> c. 36% Hot water (160 degrees Fahrenheit); add to
> d. 0% Polygum[4] 260, or Keltex[5] gum, cool and add
> e. 10% Sodium sulfoxylate (1:1)
>
> ———————
> 100%

After the cloth is discharge-printed, it is finished as outlined in (II) for white discharge printing on cotton.

IV. DISCHARGE PRINTING OF ACID COLORS ON SILK AND WOOL

The following is a suggested general formula[6]:

> a. 1-5% Color
> b. 1-5% Urea
> c. 40-48% Water
> d. 50% Hydro Gum and gum tragacanth paste

The Hydro Gum in the latter formulation consists of:

> a. 30% Hydrosulphite NF
> b. 10% Water
> c. 60% Gum tragacanth paste
>
> ———————
> 100%

[4] Polymer Industries, Inc., New York, NY
[5] Kelco Co., Clark, NJ
[6] Ciba-Geigy Corp., Greensboro, NC

The proportion of Hydro Gum and gum tragacanth paste must be adjusted so that the final print paste contains the necessary amount of Hydrosulphite to discharge the ground color. The amount of Hydrosulphite may vary from five to fifteen percent.

To discharge print on wool, to prevent tendering and to obtain clear colors, it is advisable to add to the print paste the following mixture consisting of:

a. 10% zinc oxide (1:1)
b. 5% Acetine or 5% Albatex L.

The prints are either aged for ten minutes, or aged for five minutes and then steamed for fifteen to 30 minutes without pressure or with low pressure. Then the prints are rinsed in a cold solution containing two grams of hydrogen peroxide per liter, soaped for a few minutes at 90 degrees Fahrenheit, rinsed and soured in a cold solution of two grams of acetic acid (56%) and one gram of Fixacol per liter, and are finally extracted and dried.

V. WHITE DISCHARGES ON WOOL AND SILK DYED WITH ACID DYESTUFFS

The following is the discharge recipe[7]:

a. 250 parts Redusol Z are pasted with
b. 100 parts blood albumen (40% solution)
c. 80 parts glycerin and
d. 200 parts titanium dioxide (50%) paste.
      This mixture is stirred into
e. 270 parts of gum tragacanth (7%) thickening

_____

Bulk to 1000 parts

The titanium dioxide (zinc oxide can be used instead of titanium dioxide) must be very finely dispersed by grinding it with a small proportion of water and thickening, and adding it to the print paste. Up to twenty percent of titanium or zinc oxide may be incorporated in the discharge paste to improve the quality of discharging on dyed ground shades of silk and especially on wool.

After printing, the cloth is dried, steamed for ten to fifteen minutes in steam that is as air-free as possible and washed in cold water.

[7] Imperial Chemical Industries Limited, Manchester, England

VI. COLOR DISCHARGE PRINTING WITH BASIC DYESTUFF ON WOOL AND SILK DYED GROUNDS

The following is the discharge formula[7]:
a. 20 parts dyestuff are pasted with
b. 50 parts Glydote BN and to this are added
c. 250 parts hot water. When the mixture is cool
d. 150 parts Formosul are added.
      The mixture is stirred into
e. 530 parts gum tragacanth (7%) thickening.

Bulk to 1000 parts.

The cloth is discharge-printed, dried lightly in a hot-air stove and steamed for ten minutes at 212 degrees Fahrenheit. It is then rinsed, soaped lightly, rinsed again and dried.

Regardless of the discharge product the printer is attempting to use, he must realize that he not only buys a specific product but also a process. Therefore, he must standardize his processing and keep careful notes of all his work, especially at first, so that he will obtain the same results, using the same procedures and products, each time. It is suggested that the printer attempt regular textile screen printing before the more challenging discharge printing.

142

Chapter XVI

FLOCKING AND TEXTILE SCREEN PRINTING

It is interesting to note that flocking, or decorating an adhesive-covered surface with very short fibers, was originally employed to imitate fabrics. Flocking to produce wall decorations was used in the 14th Century—very short lengths of fibers were applied with bellows to freshly-painted wall areas to produce a fabric effect. However, flocking as a commercial enterprise, using fibers such as viscose rayon, cotton, acrylic polyester, fluorocarbon or wool are now offered for industrial use with exacting quality and maintenance of standards. These fibers really developed after World War I.

In the 1920s some firms doing flocking built their own equipment for applying flock to adhesive-covered surfaces. Some even used simple flocking units with beater bars rotating at fairly high speeds against a blanket over which the flocked items passed. The vibration caused by the beater bars (similar to today's vibration machines) made the flock fibers jump and become embedded in the adhesive.

Typical flocked products include such items as drapery material, sports and dress apparel, T-shirts, upholstery and bedspread coverings. Also, today flock may be applied to paper or cardboard, and on such substrates as plastics, foam material, wood and metals. Flock can be applied on regular or irregular shapes.

In screen printing, flocking has been used both as a process to supplement general screen printing and as a specialized phase. Specifically, flocking is a process in which finely-cut, very short fibers are applied to a surface upon which an adhesive has been coated. The adhesive can be applied by screen-printing, by passing the material through a roller coating machine, by using spray guns, by hand-brushing or by dipping;

143

in textile printing the first two methods are used most often.

Flock may be applied over a whole surface or it may be applied in a repeat design form. It can be adhered to a flat surface or applied to a surface that is in a vertical position, allowing one end of the flock fiber to stick out in the air. It can also be applied on both sides of a fabric or substrate, with the fabric being printed between two identical printing screens arranged vertically.

While flock is usually applied directly to a substrate, it can also be processed onto certain surfaces to be used as transfers. Transfers can be made by applying flock on one side of a foil and a thermoplastic adhesive on the other. The printed designs are die-cut from the flocked and printed sheet, and applied with heat and pressure later. Many small designs can be cut from the same sheet, and the designs may be processed before they are actually needed.

Flock consists of fine short strands or filaments precision-cut into controlled lengths varying from 1/2mm (.0197 inch) to about 1/4 inch. Flock may be used to cover any surface upon which an adhesive can be applied. It is available in white, in all colors and also in fluorescent colors. The most popular lengths are 1/16 inch and 1/32 inch.

Since 1960 the growth of flocking has accelerated and produced new end products in the decoration of textiles just as it has in other fields. This growth has been brought about by more practical methods of flock-cutting on the part of the flock manufacturers, by more practical applications of the flock, by the fact that flock has proven to be a durable finish, by the availability of a variety of adhesives and by the technical information made available by manufacturers and suppliers. However, because screen printing produces an individuality of flock designs not possible with other processes and because it prints a heavy adhesive deposit, it is being used more and more in textile flock-printing. Flock is used to produce a variety of materials and products such as nylon automobile upholstery, indoor and outdoor carpeting, shoe fabrics, certain areas of girdles, women's ski pants, car coats and jackets, polyethylene film for draperies and cafe curtains, gloves and hats, for simulating suede and velvet-like fabrics, for producing designs resembling embroidery on dress material, sportswear, handbags, swimwear, wallpaper to match flocked drapery and jewelry boxes. Textile flocked materials are not intended as substitutes but are designed as decorated materials that withstand use.

As with all phases of textile screen printing, flocking should not be attempted on a commercial scale until the printer has experimented thoroughly with printing various adhesives on different textile materials, with flock, with printing screens, with manual, vibrating and electrostatic flocking, with drying equipment, and with flocking one flock color on

144

another flock color. Generally, the design patterns on textile materials are screen-printed with an adhesive through a printing screen, either manually, semi-automatically or with completely automatic equipment. Some textile-printing plants use rotary and flat screen- printing machines for applying the adhesive. Flock usually remains on the surface by penetrating the adhesive; pigments and dyes penetrate the textile fiber. In screen printing, the fabric material with the adhesive-printed pattern passes under a hopper that contains the correct flock and color which is then applied onto the wet printed design. The flocked design then passes onto a conveyor from the hopper, over bars known as beater or spanking bars (see Figure 72 and 73) and then to a dryer.

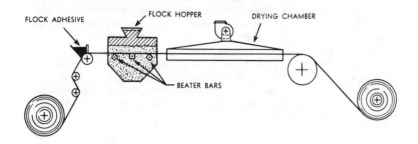

Figure 72. Diagram of the operation of a vibration type flocking machine. When flock-printing on textiles, the designs are applied with printing screens rather than with rollers. (Courtesy of Cellusuede Products, Inc., Rockford, IL)

Figure 73. A detail drawing of a beater or vibration bar. (Courtesy of Cellusuede Products, Inc., Rockford, IL)

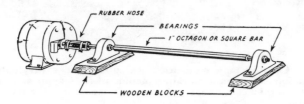

When applying flock, whether it is done manually or automatically, the processor must ensure that the flock is not blown about the room and that, to prevent health hazards, it is removed from the air which the operator breathes. It is suggested, especially if homemade equipment is used, that the operator wear at least a simple respiratory mask to prevent breathing in the flock. Masks and other such items are available from flock and screen process suppliers. Not only should the printer watch his health, he should also attempt to eliminate the loss of flock by using a reclaiming system. This may be done with gravity—the flock that falls to the bottom of the flocking booth or conveyor is reclaimed with a vacuum device similar to that used in an ordinary vacuum cleaner. With specifically designed automatic flocking equipment the loss of flock and contamination of the air are held to a minimum. For example, in electrostatic flocking machines, the flock is applied onto the item without the operator touching it from the moment it is registered for printing until it is removed from the machine completely flocked. These units, which are fully enclosed flocking machines, have a means for recirculating the flock, provide quick cleaning when changing flock colors, have a device for removing excess flock at the exit end of the unit and may be designed and built to suit the size, shape and weight of the product to be flocked (see Figures 74, 75 and 77).

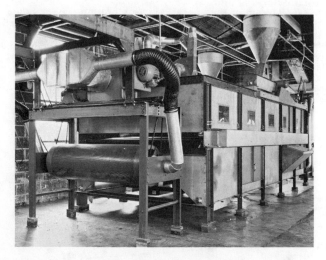

Figure 74. A custom-built automatic flocking machine which employs a combination electrostatic-vibration method of flock application for flock-printing on a continuous web or textile material. Adhesives may be applied by screen-printing or with engraved rollers.
(Courtesy of Indev, Inc., Pawtucket, RI)

146

Figure 75. A 5-Color-MC-Automatic Flock Machine which produces multicolor flock designs directly on the required surface. (Courtesy of Kopal Industries, Inc., Seabrook, TX)

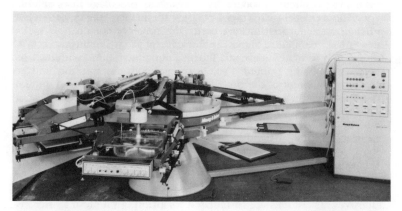

Figure 76. The Femco electrostatic flocking unit used for flocking a variety of materials and objects, simplifies clean-up, keeps the flock in a compartment and permits color changes of flock in a very short period of time. (Courtesy of Flocking Equipment Manufacturing Co., Los Angeles, CA)

147

Adhesives

The correct application of the proper adhesive on the textile material is the first important step in flocking. Flock adhesives usually dry slowly and should dry from the center outward. Adhesives can be applied by screen-printing, roller textile machine-printing, plain roller-printing or by spraying. The adhesive used depends on the type of material being flocked, the method of flock application, the method of drying and the end use of the flocked product. Various adhesives such as water-soluble types, alkyd enamels, vinyl types, acrylics, synthetic rubber-types, screen-printing inks and plastisols are used. The adhesive must remain tacky or wet long enough to allow the flock fibers to anchor firmly into it. It must also be of a type that will form a permanent bond with the textile material being printed. Usually the color of the adhesive will be similar to the color of the flock being applied. Adhesives used on textiles must meet laundering and dry cleaning requirements; therefore, it is not an easy task for the processor to prepare adhesives. Some adhesives must be flexible and some rigid; some must resist water and solvents and some must withstand heat and cold.

Plastisol is a practical ink or adhesive developed especially for screen-printing on textiles (see Chapter XII). Plastisols, stretch inks or rubber-type inks are plastic-type screen-printing inks also used as flocking adhesives. These inks are formulated for printing on mesh fabrics, T-shirts, denim material, cotton and similar materials. They adhere excellently to the fabric and produce a highly embossed, elastic, opaque and wash-fast coating. The flock may be applied to these adhesives electrostatically, with beater bars or manually. Plastisols may be screened through 6XX silk or an equivalent screen fabric using a heavy stencil, and a soft or textile squeegee for printing on textile material. The material to be printed can be placed on a soft base such as felt or rubber. These inks or adhesives should be thoroughly mixed before use and should be stored in a cool area (below 100 degrees Fahrenheit, 38C); high temperatures may result in jelling of the ink.

Because of the variety of fabric finishes, it is suggested that the adhesive be pretested on the material to be printed, flocked and dried. After this type of adhesive is printed and flocked, the material must be baked at 240 to 325 degrees Fahrenheit (116 to 163 degrees Celsius) for about three to eight minutes, the lower the temperature used, the longer the curing time. Heat from infrared lamps or gas ovens may be used for baking. The curing time is reduced slightly for darker shades. Plastisols are thermoplastics; they soften with the application of heat. Therefore, printed fabrics should be ironed with a moderately warm iron. With some plastisols, the flocked design area should be pressed from the back side or pressed with a cover cloth over the printed textile material. The flocked material will resist washing after the adhesive and the flock have been heat-cured. This information applies to plastisols; other adhesives will differ.

148

The printer must ensure that the printed and flocked garment is properly labeled. The consumer must be instructed in proper laundering procedures.

The advantage of screen-printing the adhesive is that it will be applied in a thicker coating than it would be with other processes. Also, the printed design is uniform in thickness. Generally, the longer the flock, the thicker the adhesive coating needs to be. Coarser screen fabrics should be used on the printing screens which are to print the adhesive. Screen fabrics may vary from Number 2 silk or its equivalent to about Number 8. The same mesh should be used when applying the same pattern on bolt material. The printing screens used are similar to those used in textile or general screen printing. Of course, the screen used must resist the adhesive and the solvents in the adhesive. Usually knife-cut films and photographic screens are employed for printing adhesive designs. With automatic screen-printing textile machines, the adhesive can be applied in any size or any type of repeat pattern onto bolt or piece material for automatic flock application.

Flock Application

The most used methods of commercial flock application in textile screen printing are hand-sifting, spraying flock onto the adhesive-covered surface, using a vibrating machine or employing electrostatic attraction. The latter two methods are used for mechanical flocking onto bolt material and for single-piece flocking. In spray flocking, the flock is sprayed onto the already applied adhesive. The printer who has to flock only an occasional job may even apply flock onto the adhesive with homemade sifters, in a similar fashion to that done by earlier processors. However, custom-built machines for flock-printing on textiles cater to the electrostatic method, the vibration or beater bar method or a combination of the two. The combination method is the preferred method of application.

The vibration, beater bar or spanking bar method (Figures 72 and 73) is usually used for flocking piece goods, flat objects and flat surfaces. Individual flat objects and bolts of material can be conveyed over beater bars. In this method the adhesive is coated onto the material by screen-printing the design onto it; the material is then passed under a flock hopper where the flock is automatically dropped onto it; and the material is moved over the beater bars either at the same time it is flocked or immediately after. The beater bars, which are hexagonal or square shaped (about one to three inches in cross section), are rotated at about 600 to 1700 revolutions per minute. Another type of beater bar has leather straps wrapped around the bar with the conveyor passing over the leather producing the vibrating action. The bars are perpendicular to the motion of the conveyor and the movement of the screen-processed pieces. The revolutions per minute can be varied according to the requirements of different materials and projects.

The beater bars beat on the underside of the conveyor blanket on which the object has been placed, causing the object or material to vibrate while the flock is being applied onto its surface. The vibration causes the flock to become deeply embedded in the adhesive. At the same time, an electrostatic field is created by the friction, which causes the fiber to stick upright in the adhesive. The processor should make sure that the fibers are not flocked onto the surface before the vibrators are in action.

As soon as the flocking is completed, the material passes through a dryer, or in the case of single textile items, the products may be allowed to dry naturally on racks or are exposed to infrared heat on a conveyor. The fabric may be festoon-dried or loop-dried to prevent offsetting or mark-off, and may be brushed after drying to remove loose flock. Drying may be accomplished naturally or may be accelerated by using low-temperature heat of about 150 degrees Fahrenheit (66 degrees Celsius). The type of adhesive used will determine to what extent heat can be used. If conveyor blankets carry the bolt material or items under infrared heat, it is suggested that the material not be allowed to get too hot. The movement of the conveyor should be synchronized with the infrared unit so that when the conveyor stops the infrared heat will be turned off automatically to prevent burning the textile flocked material. The drying equipment used is dependent on the average material which will be flocked in the shop. There are adhesives which dry by means of oxidation and do not require heat-curing; there are others which are heat-cured. The manufacturer of the adhesive will recommend the most practical method of drying.

Electrostatic flocking is possible because of the simple law of physics which states that like electrical charges repel each other and opposite charges attract each other. In practice, electrostatic flocking consists of having two electrodes (conductors) with a high potential difference or voltage between them, one with a positive charge and the other a negative charge. An electrostatic field is created between the positive and negative electrode, furnishing the force of attraction. As the flock is introduced into this field, it becomes electrically charged and is attracted to the plate or the adhesive of the opposite charge. The adhesive screen-printed material is positioned to intercept these electrically charged fibers which are impelled at high-speed and penetrate the adhesive, becoming vertically positioned. The adhesive on the material is grounded electrically.

The force acting on each flock particle becomes greater as the charge increases, and the strength of the electrostatic field increases as the voltage increases. On the other hand, as the distance between the electrodes increases the force decreases. The voltage of flocking machines may be as high as 150,000 volts. Either alternating or direct current can be used. There are a variety of electrostatic flocking machines. Some propel the flock downward and some upward. As with the beater-bar method, although the machines may seem complex, they are safe and easy to operate. It is interesting to note that when printing on plastics, the presence of static electricity is usually a disadvantage, while in flocking, electrostatics produce adhesion of the fiber and its placement in an erect position. Electrostatics produce a pile surface. This method is generally used to apply flock onto adhesive-printed patterns and onto narrow fabrics such as net fabric and bolt material.

Flock manufacturers supply flock that has a degree of electrical conductivity, and will generally recommend a type of adhesive which will help attract particles. Humidity in the working area must be controlled to ensure that flock moisture is not lost during the electrostatic flocking.

As shown in Figure 77, the material which has been screen-printed with the correct adhesive is passed automatically under the flock hopper where the precisely cut flock enters the electrostatic field and is impelled onto the electrostatically charged adhesive on the material which is moving on a conveyor. The excess flock is recovered with a pneumatic device, and the flocked fabric proceeds to a drying chamber and is heat-cured if necessary.

Excess dry flock must be removed by brushing or vacuuming, or it may fall to the sides of the conveyor belt where it can drop into troughs on each side of the unit. If the flock is clean and good housekeeping habits are employed, it may be reused. Regardless of the method of flocking used, the overfeed of flock is necessary although it should not be overdone. Excess flock should not be reused too many times because it may become frayed and bent.

Figure 77. The electrostatic method of flock application. (Courtesy of Cellusuede Products, Inc., Rockford, IL)

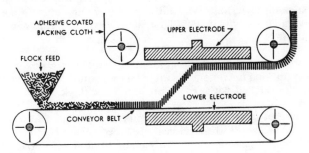

Figure 78. The R-K Automatic Flocking Machine with an L-shaped design places the machine operator between two screen-printing and flocking operations. The adhesive is printed on the garment at one position, the screen rotates out of the way and the garment flops over the electrostatic flock tray in the center while the operator screens the second garment in the second position. The machine may do 160 dozen items per day. Flocking can be done automatically or manually. (Courtesy of Cincinnati Printing & Drying Systems, Inc., Cincinnati, Ohio)

Although flocking mechanisms have built-in safety features, care must be taken that the equipment is grounded to prevent the build-up of excessive static charges which may be fire hazards, to prevent the flock from sticking to various parts of the machinery and most importantly, to prevent an arc which might ignite a fire in the solvent vapors or the flock dust.

Figure 78 presents a flocking machine that has two screen-printing and two flocking operations. Figure 79 shows cotton and velvet material which was flocked with red, white and black flock.

Because of improvements in equipment, materials and techniques, flock-printing has greatly developed and is becoming a common and very safe method of decorating not only textiles but any material to which an adhesive may be applied.

152

Figure 79. Screen-printed and flocked designs applied to cotton and velvet bolt material with white, black and red flock. (Courtesy of A-B-A Organization, Chicago, IL)

EQUIVALENT VALUES OF SOME UNITS IN THE ENGLISH (U.S.) SYSTEM OF MEASURES AND IN THE METRIC SYSTEM

Data for the following units are included should the reader have occasion to convert units from the English (U.S.) system to the metric system.

English or U.S. System	Metric System*
(1) .3937 inch	(1) 1 centimeter
(2) 1 inch	(2) 2.54 centimeters
(3) 1 inch	(3) 25.400 millimeters
(4) 39.37 inches	(4) 1 meter
(5) .0328 foot	(5) 1 centimeter
(6) 1 foot	(6) 30.48 centimerters
(7) .10936 yard	(7) 1 centimeter
(8) 1 yard	(8) 91.4402 centimeters
(9) 1 yard	(9) .9144 meter
(10) 1 point printer's measurement, .0133889 inch)	(10) .03528 centimeter
(11) 1 nonpareil (printer's measurement, 1/12 inch)	(11) .21166 centimeter
(12) 28.3441 points	(12) 1 centimeter
(13) 1 pica (printer's measurement, 1/6 inch)	(13) .42333 centimeter
(14) 1 ounce (avoirdupois)	(14) 28.3495 grams
(15) 1 pound (avoirdupois)	(15) 453.5924 grams
(16) 2.2 pounds	(16) 1 kilogram or 1000 grams
(17) 1 ounce (U.S. liquid)	(17) 29.5735 cubic centimeters
(18) 1 pint (16 ounces, U.S. fluid)	(18) .473168 liter or 473.168 cubic centimeters
(19) 1 quart (57.75 cubic inches, U.S. liquid)	(19) .946358 liter or 946.358 cubic centimeters

(20) To change Fahrenheit temperature readings *to Centigrade* readings use the following formula: (Degrees F – 32) x 5/9 = degrees Centigrade.

(21) To change Centigrade temperature readings to *Fahrenheit* readings use the following formula: (Degrees C x 9/5) + 32 = degrees Fahrenheit.

(22) To change degrees Centigrade *to Kelvin degrees* use the following formula: Degrees C + 273.1 = Kelvin temperature.

Note — Another name for the Centigrade scale is "Celsius" scale.

---

*The metric system is based on the *meter* as the unit of length, *gram* as unit of weight, and *second* as unit of time. The prefixes in the metic system are; DECI (one-tenth, .1); CENTI (one-hundredth, .01); MILLI (one-thousandth, .001); and KILO (one thousand, 1000).

Index

155

Also available from ST Publications

The ABC of Lettering
J.I. Biegeleisen

Book of 100 Type Face Alphabets
J.I. Biegeleisen

Book of 60 Hand-Lettered Alphabets
J.I. Biegeleisen

Ceramic Screen Printing
Albert Kosloff

Control Without Confusion:
Troubleshooting Screen-Printed
Process Color
Joe Clarke

57 How-To-Do-It Charts on
Materials, Equipment, Techniques
for the Screen Printer
Harry L. Hiett

Mastering Layout
Mike Stevens

Photographic Screen Printing
Albert Kosloff

Screen Printing Electronic Circuits
Albert Kosloff

Screen Printing Techniques
Albert Kosloff